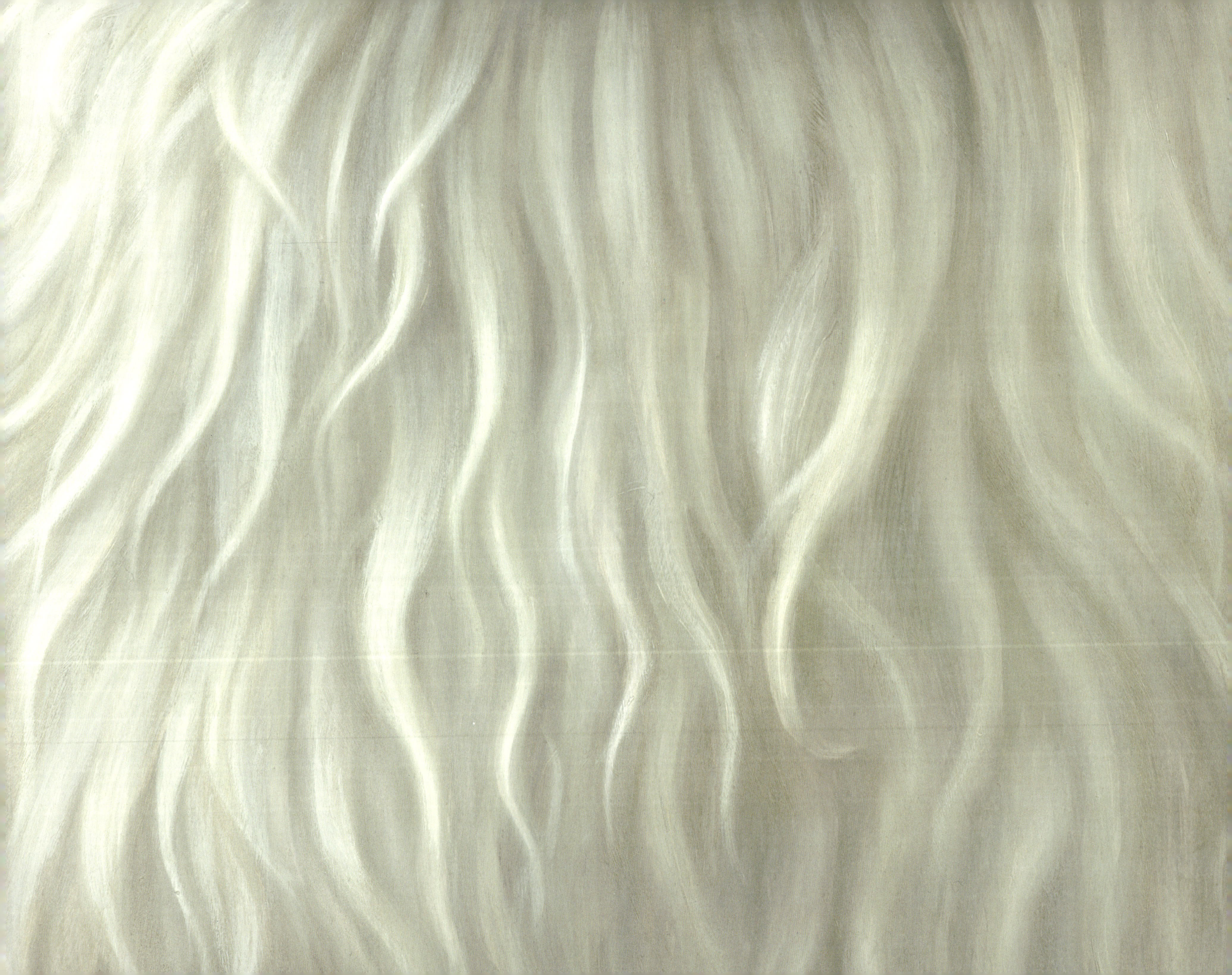

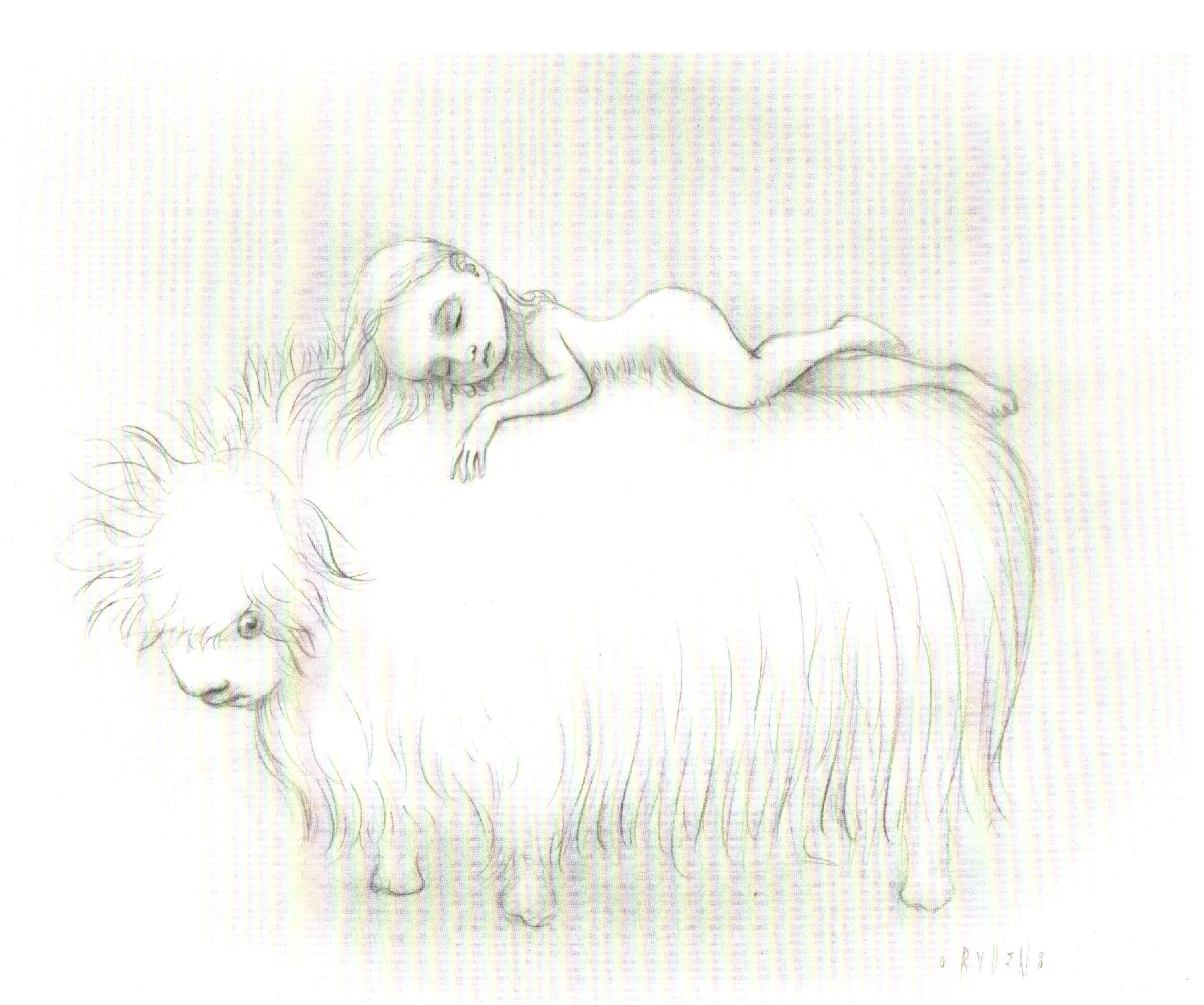

RYDENS

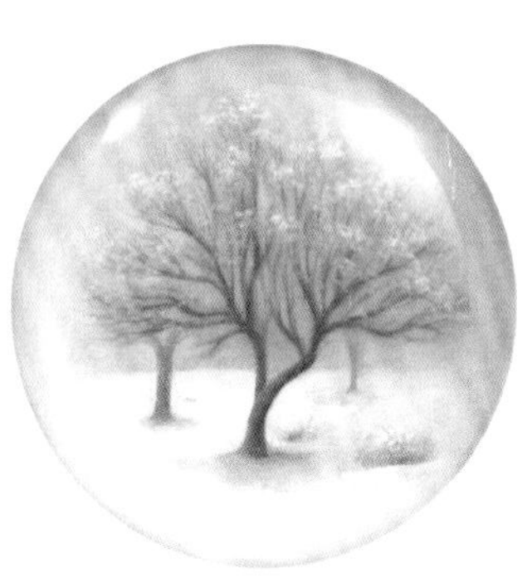

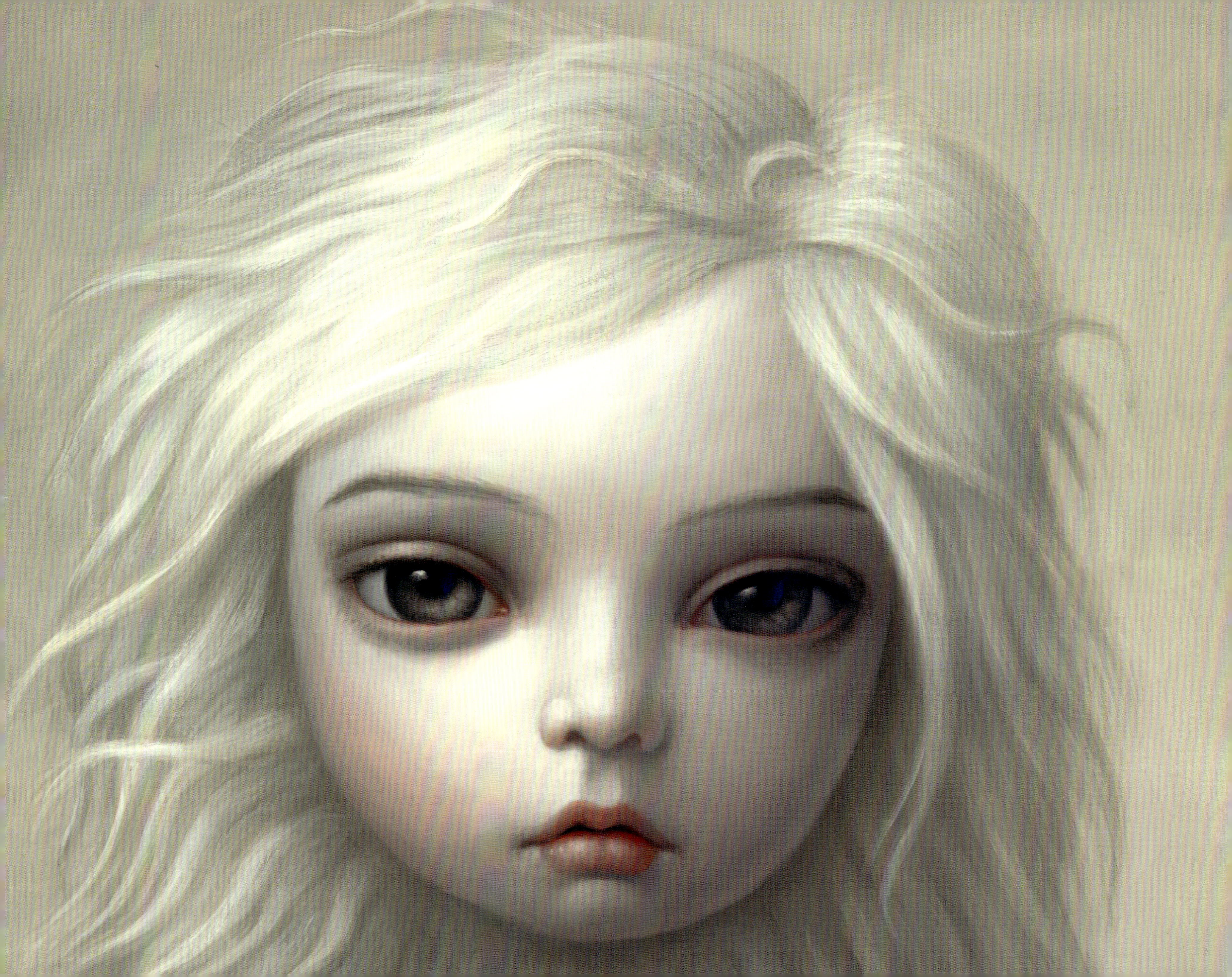

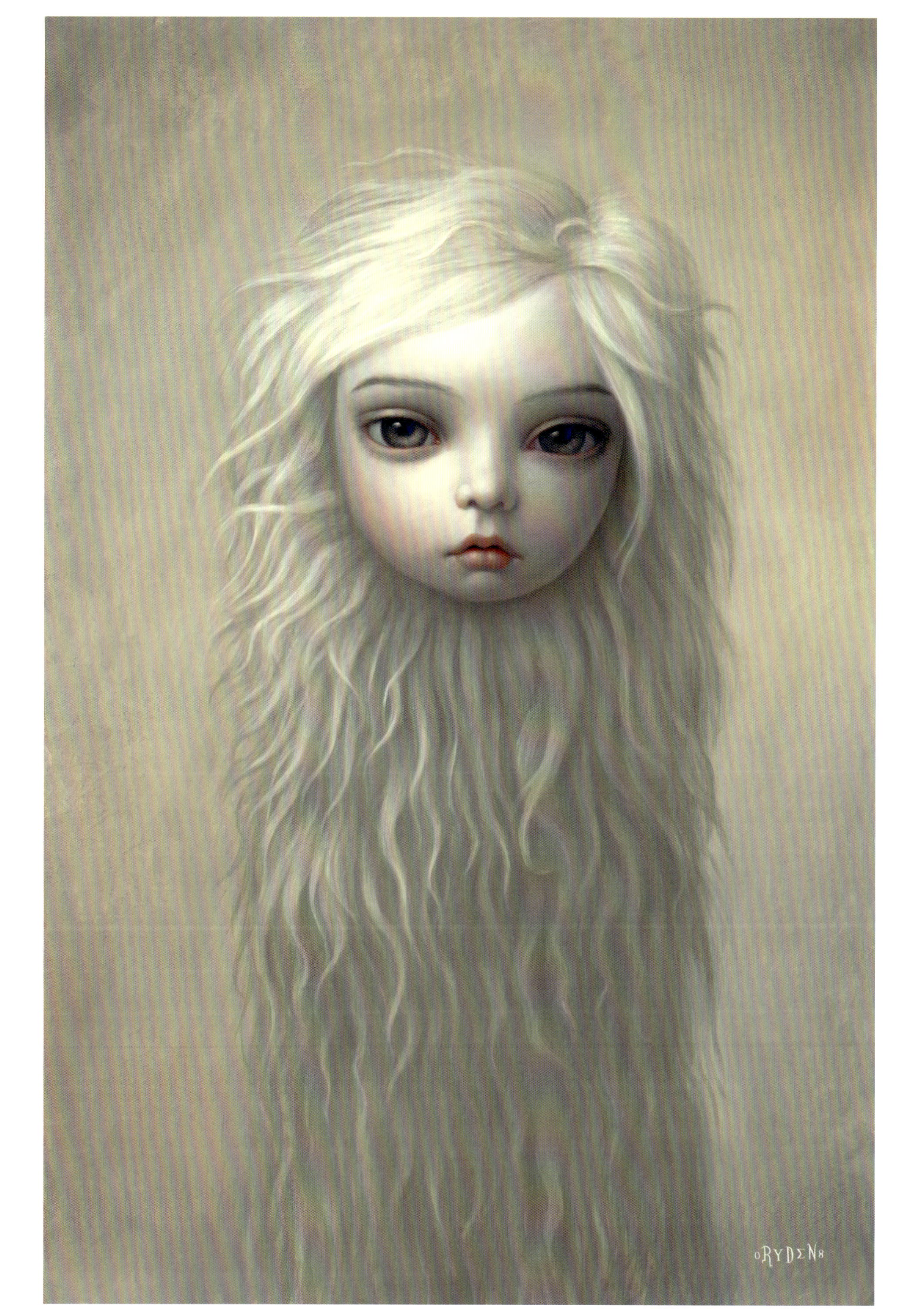

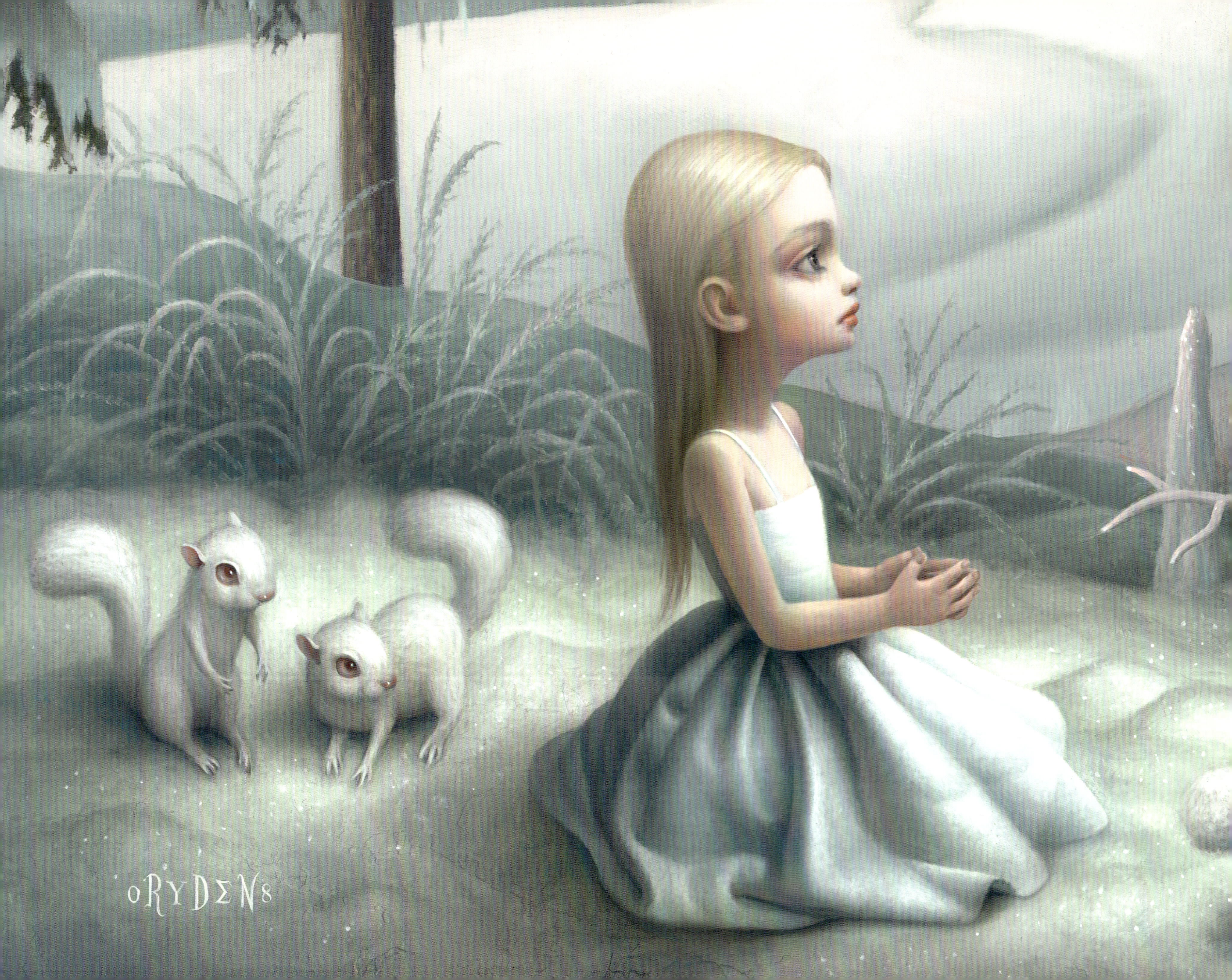
oRYDEN8

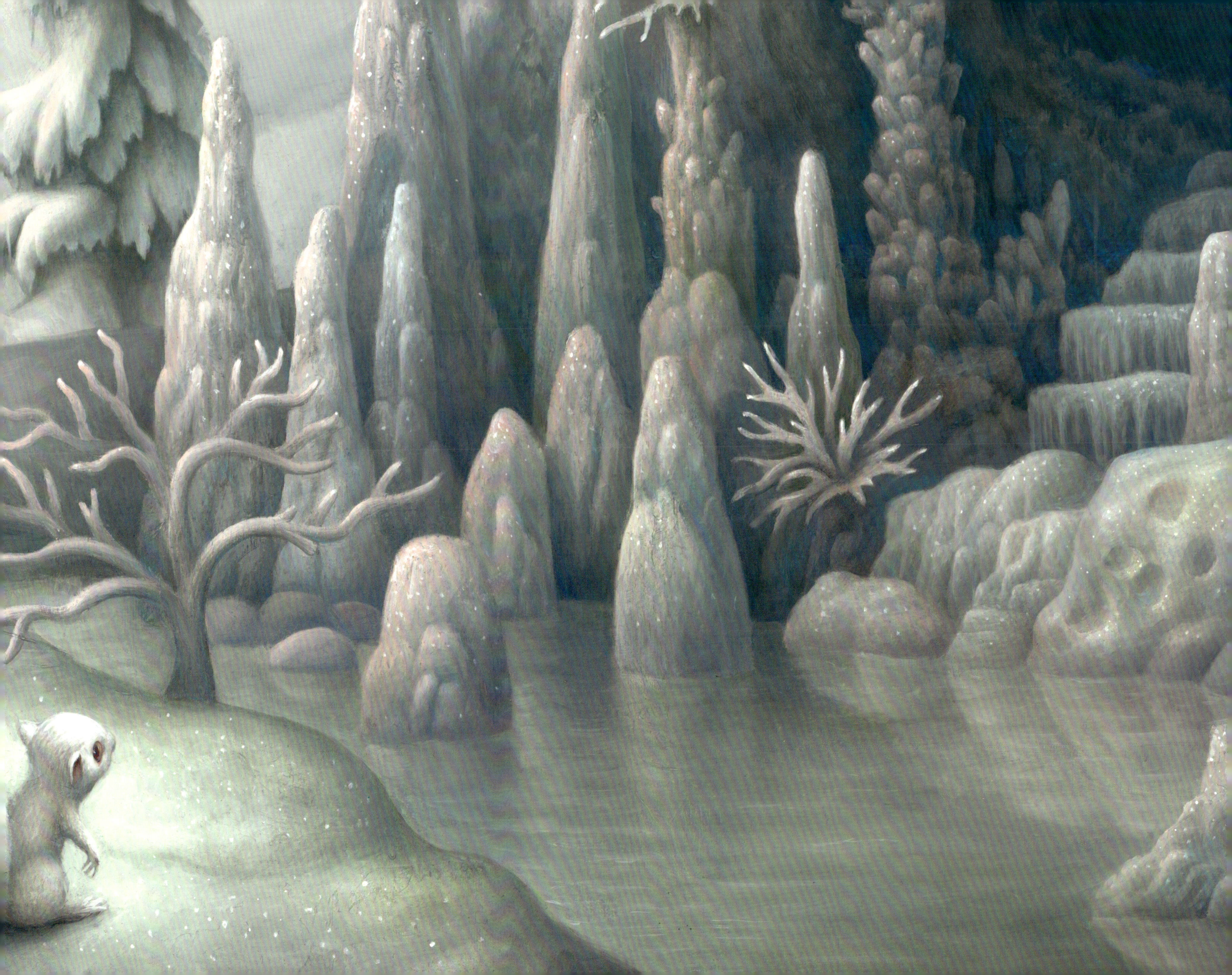

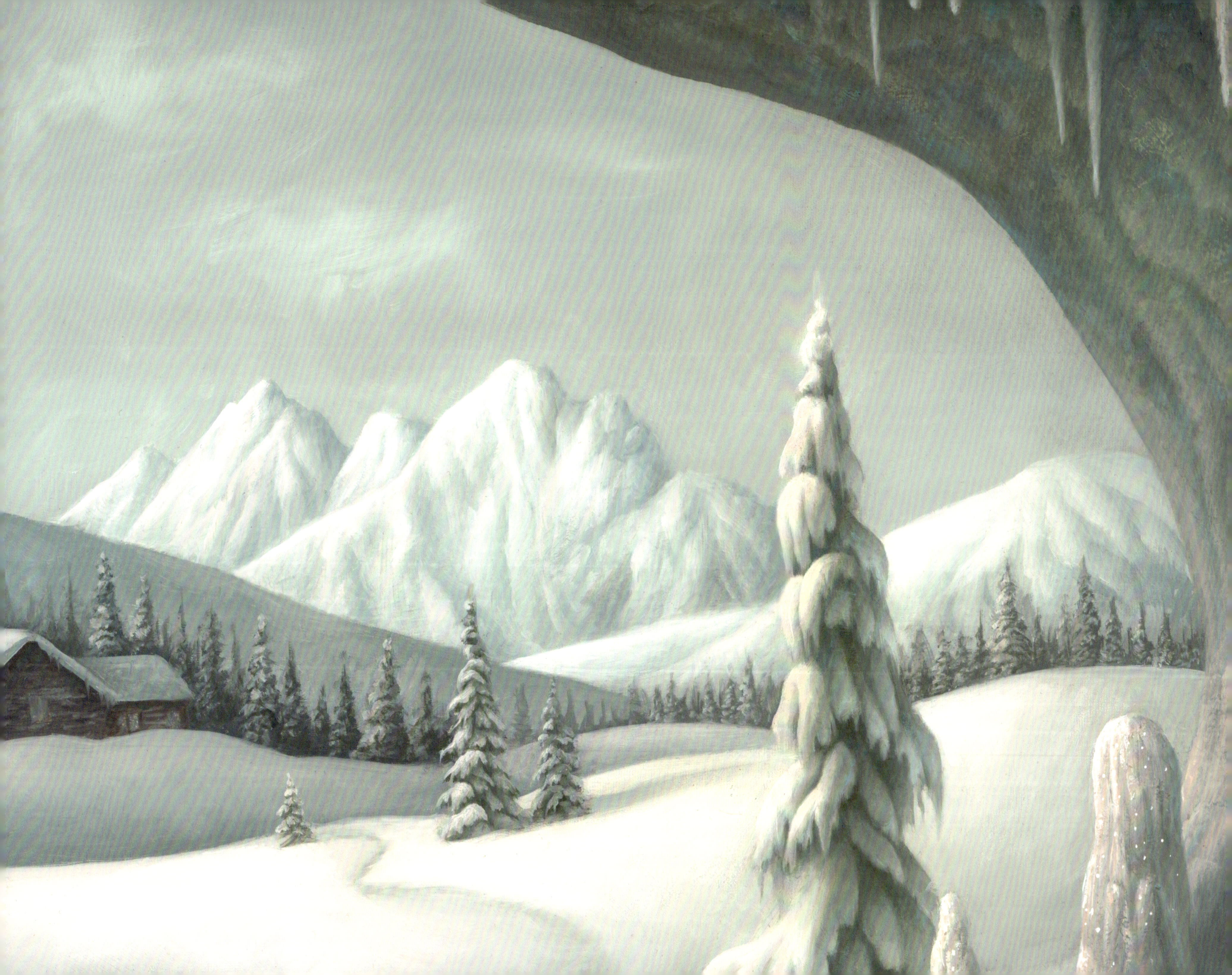

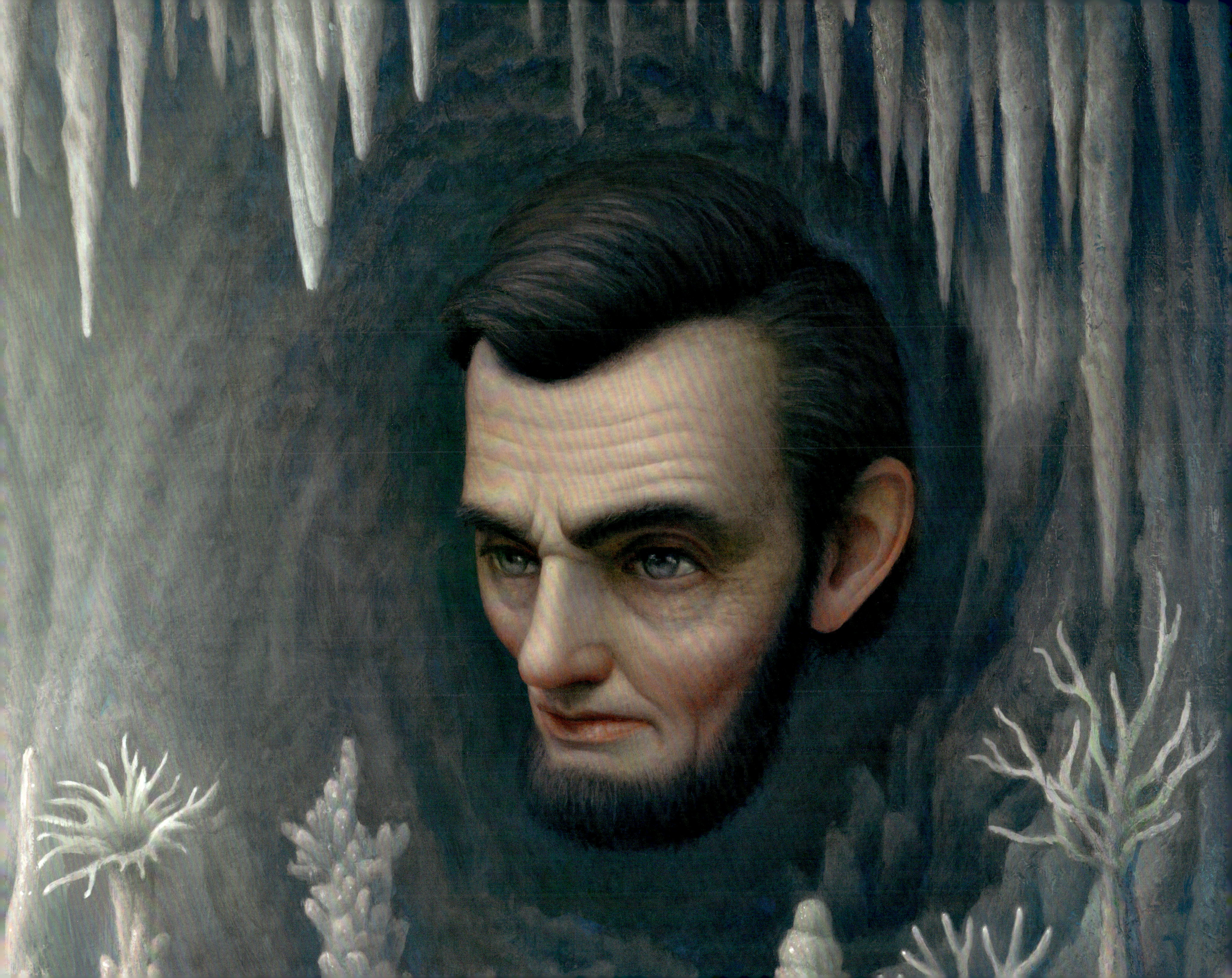

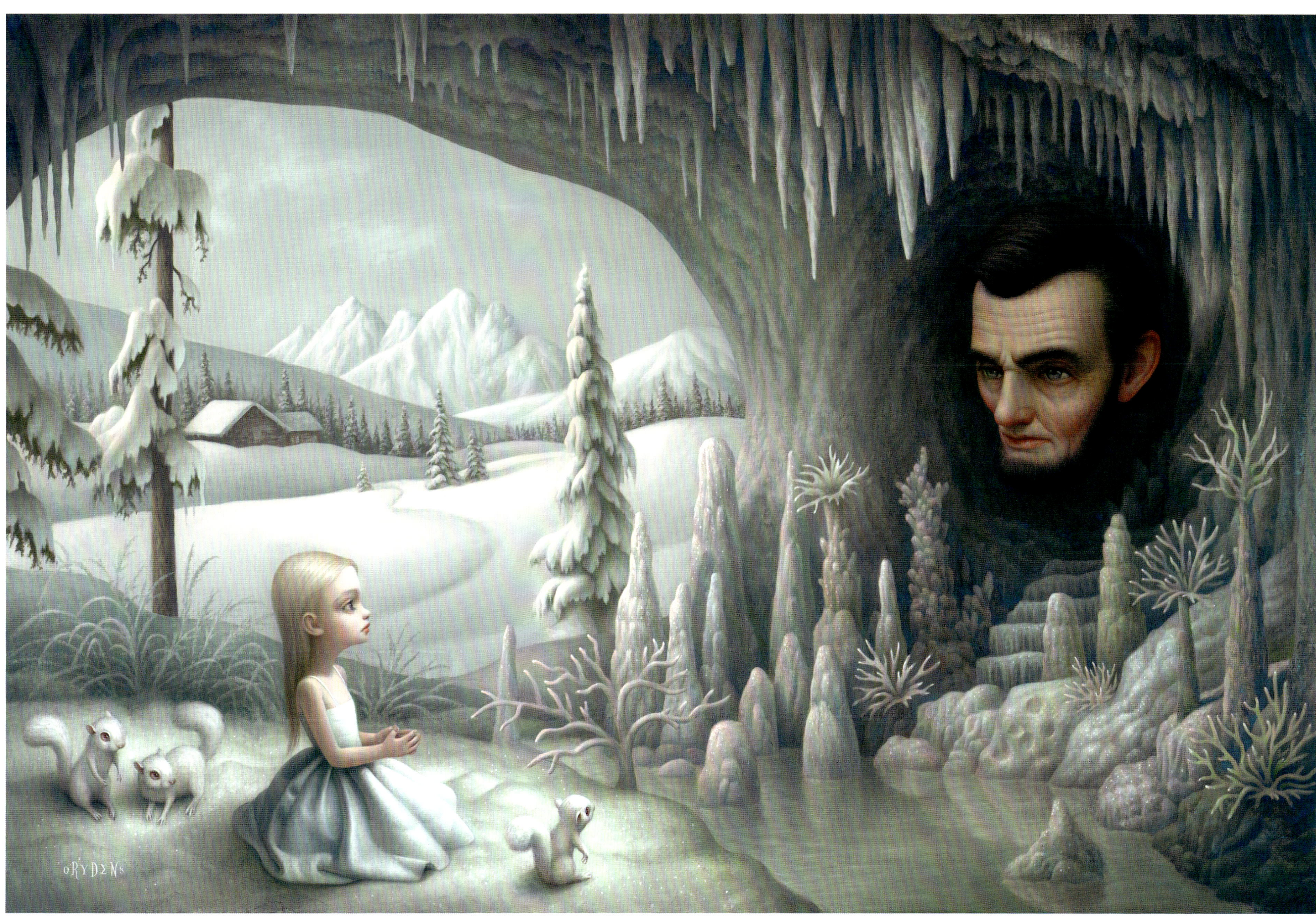

ORYDEN

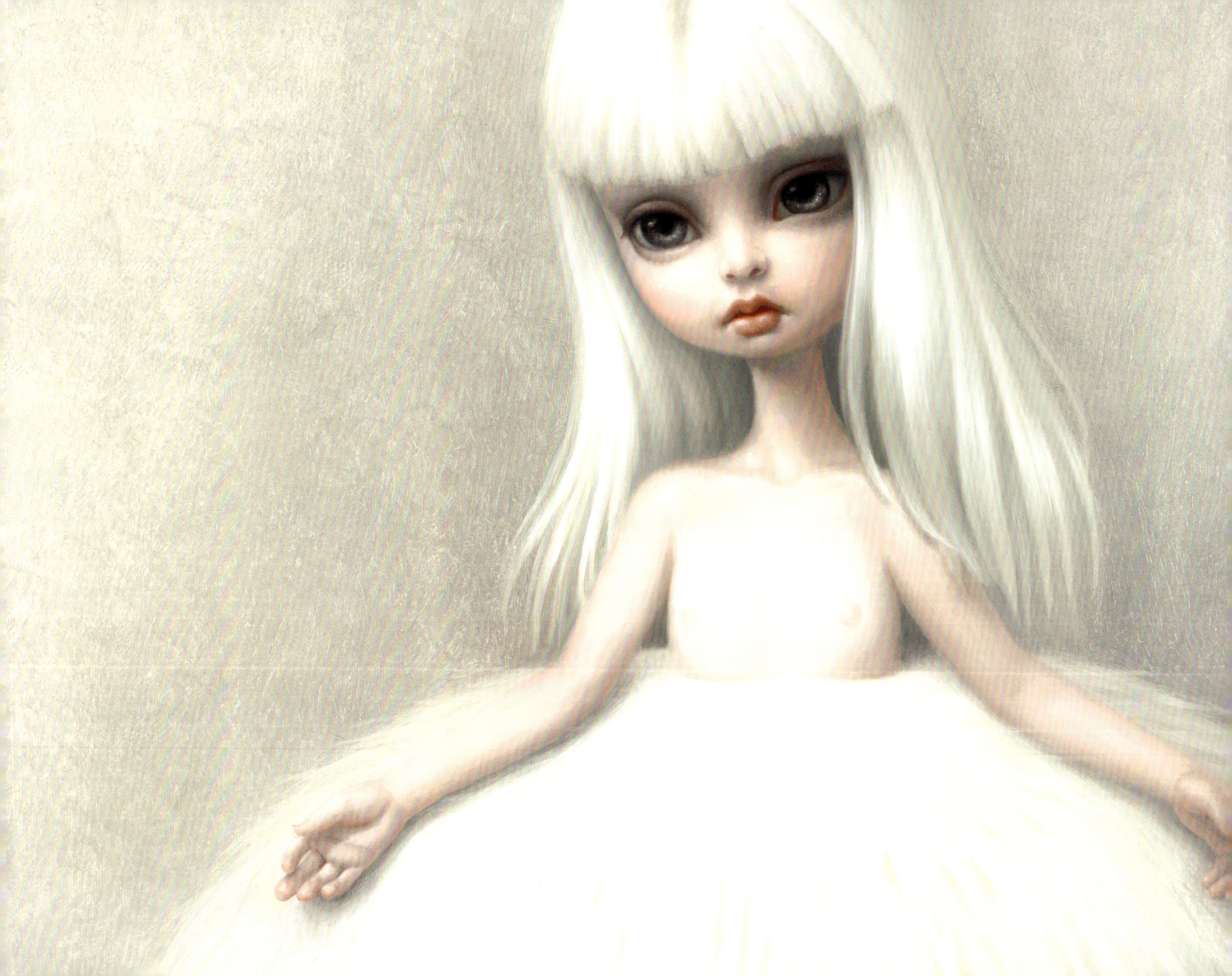

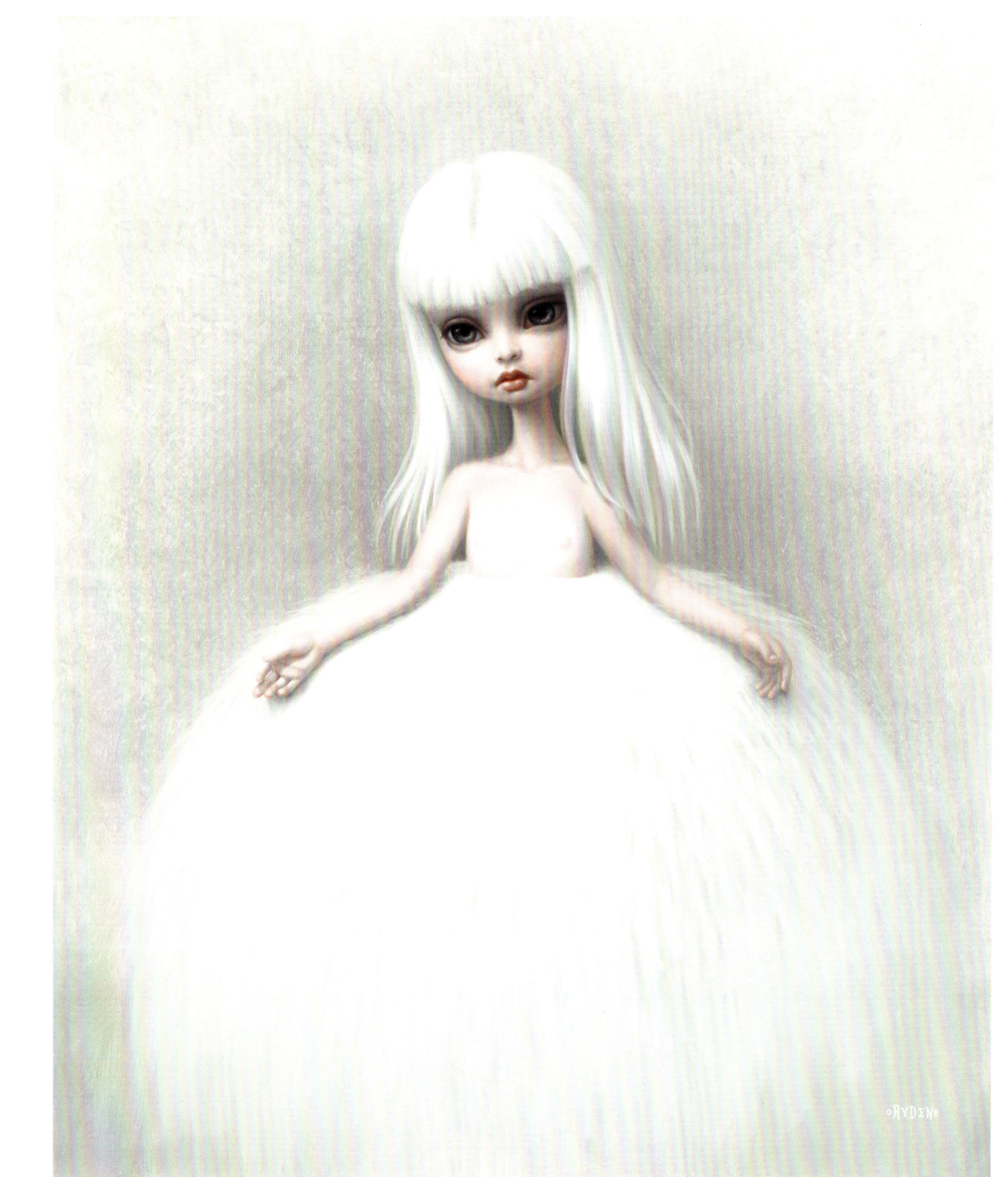
RYDEN

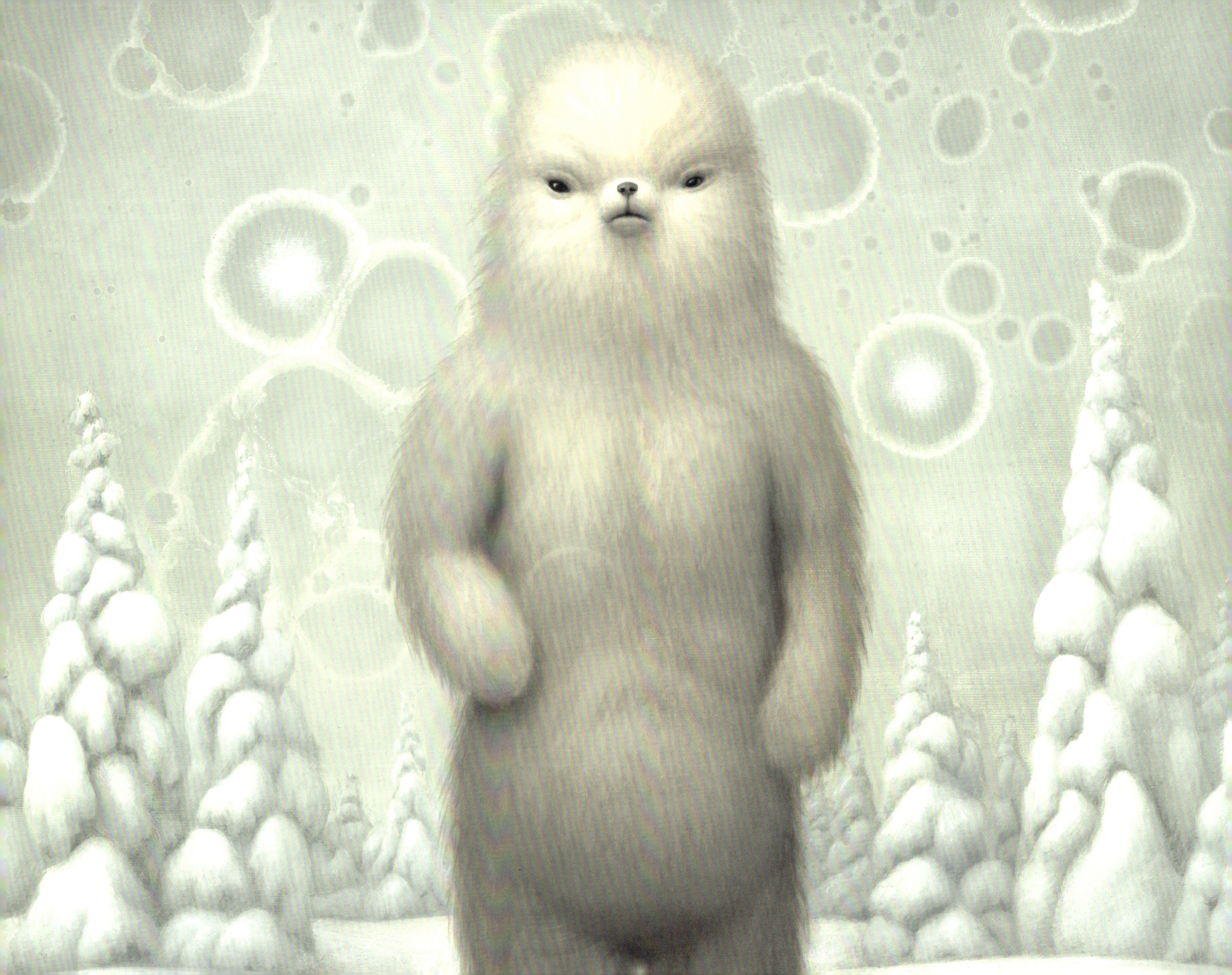

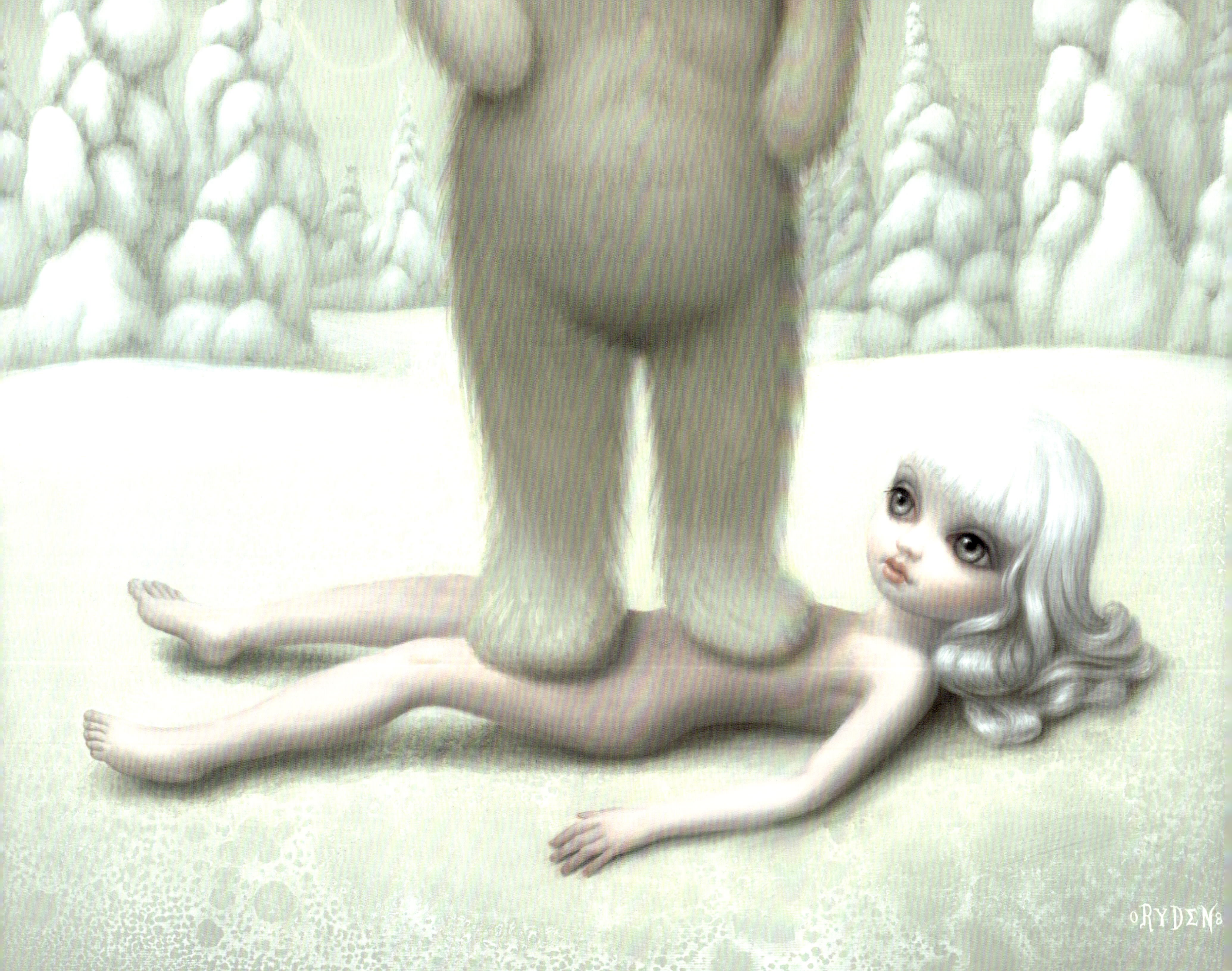

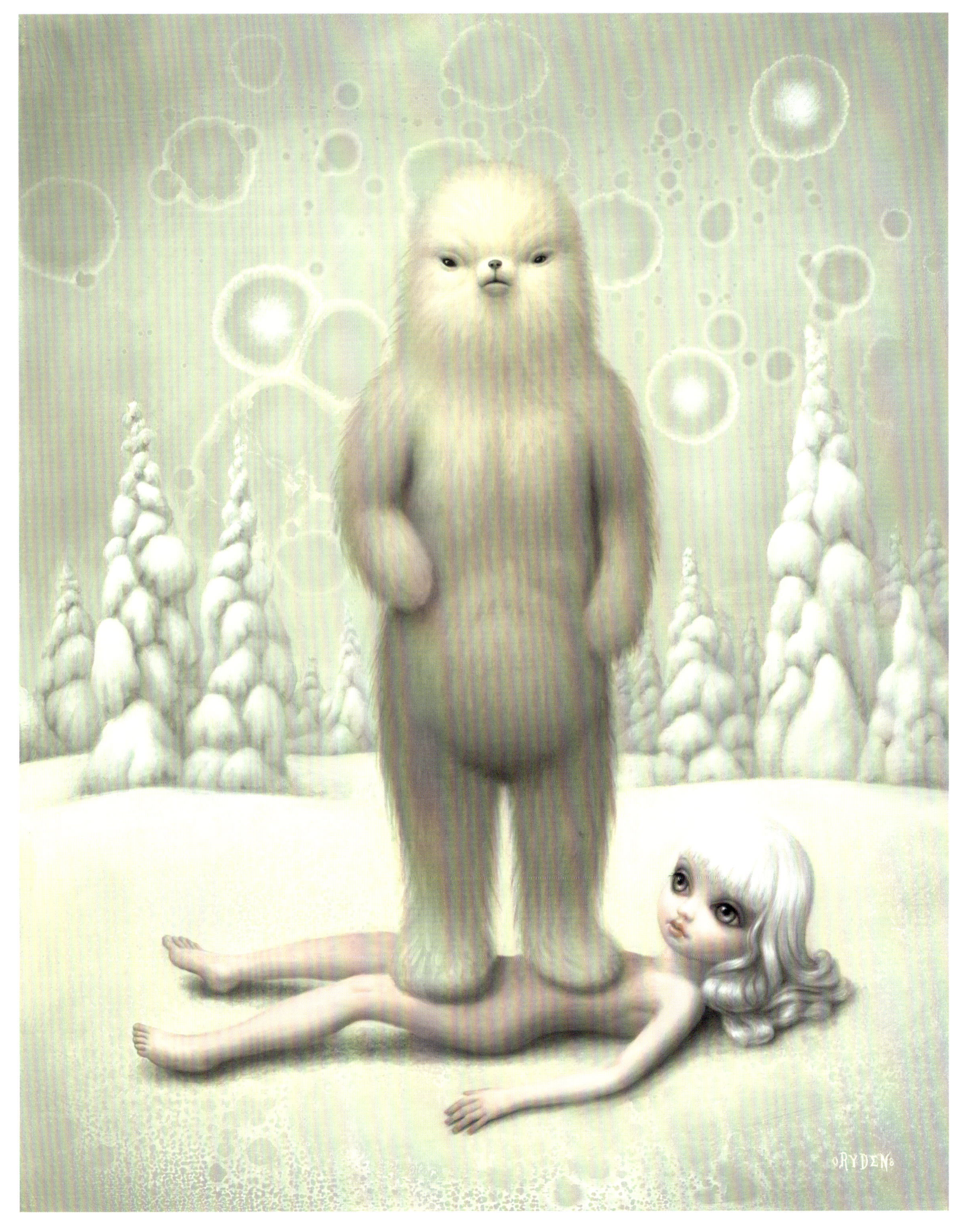
RYDEN

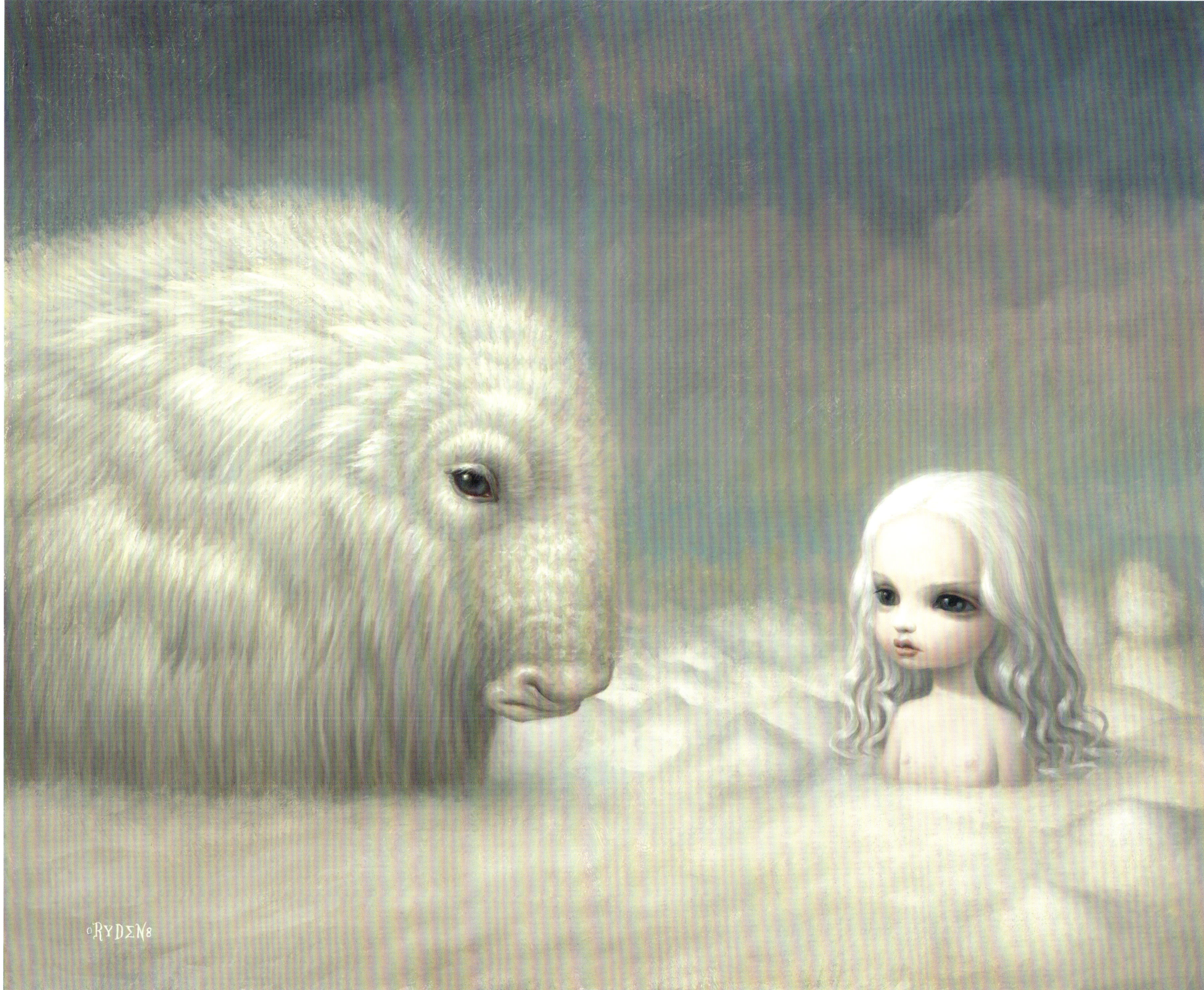

RYDEN

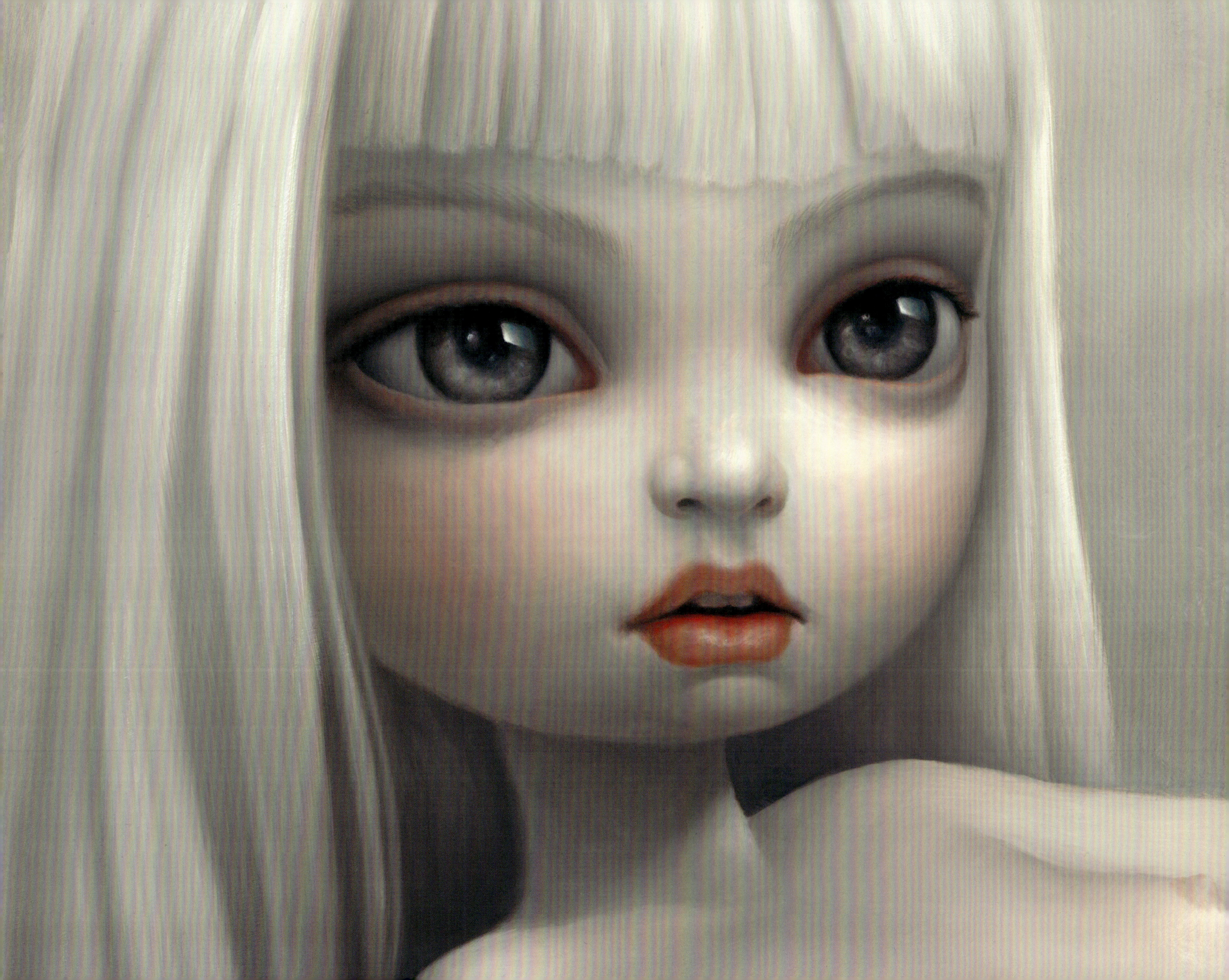

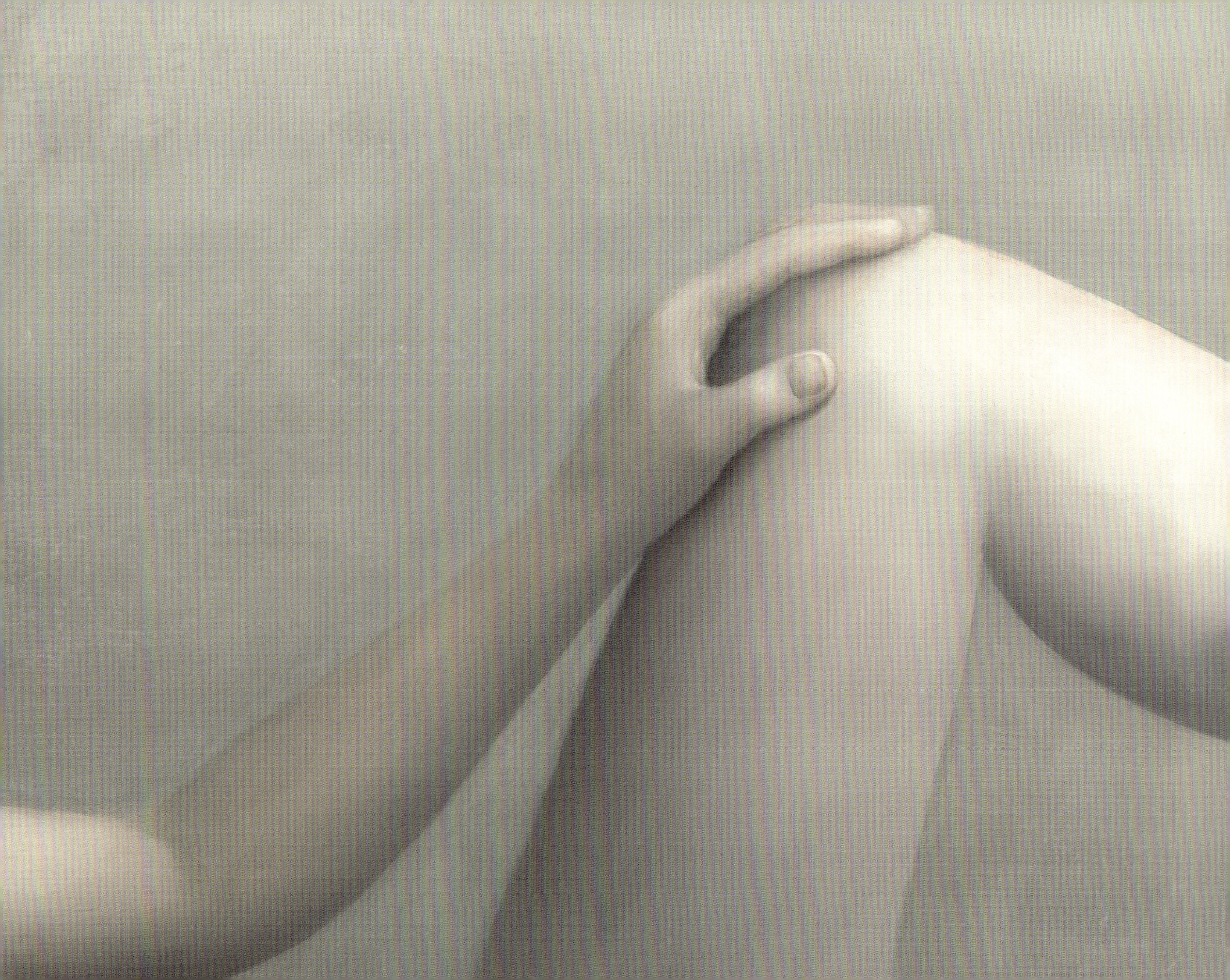

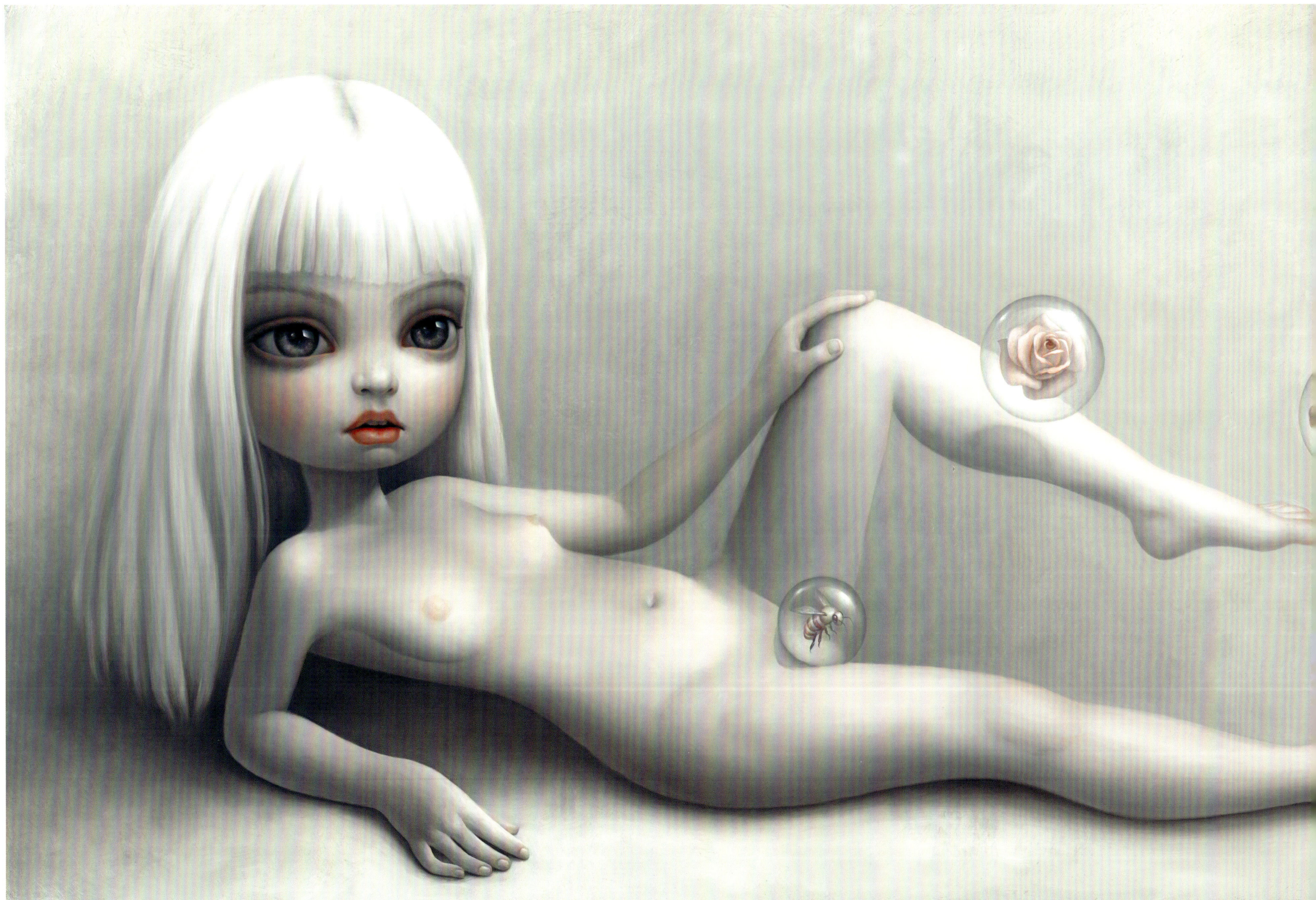

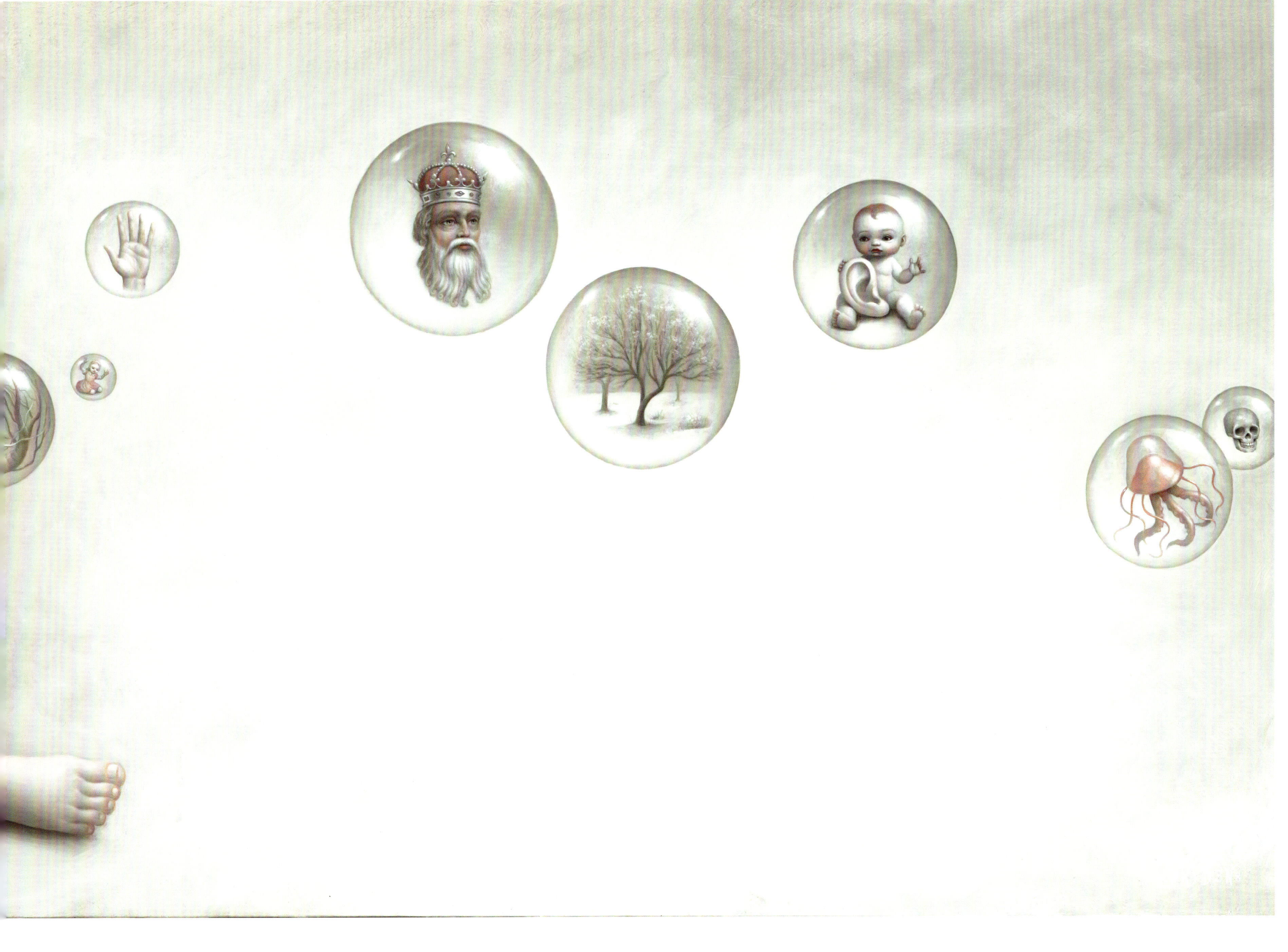

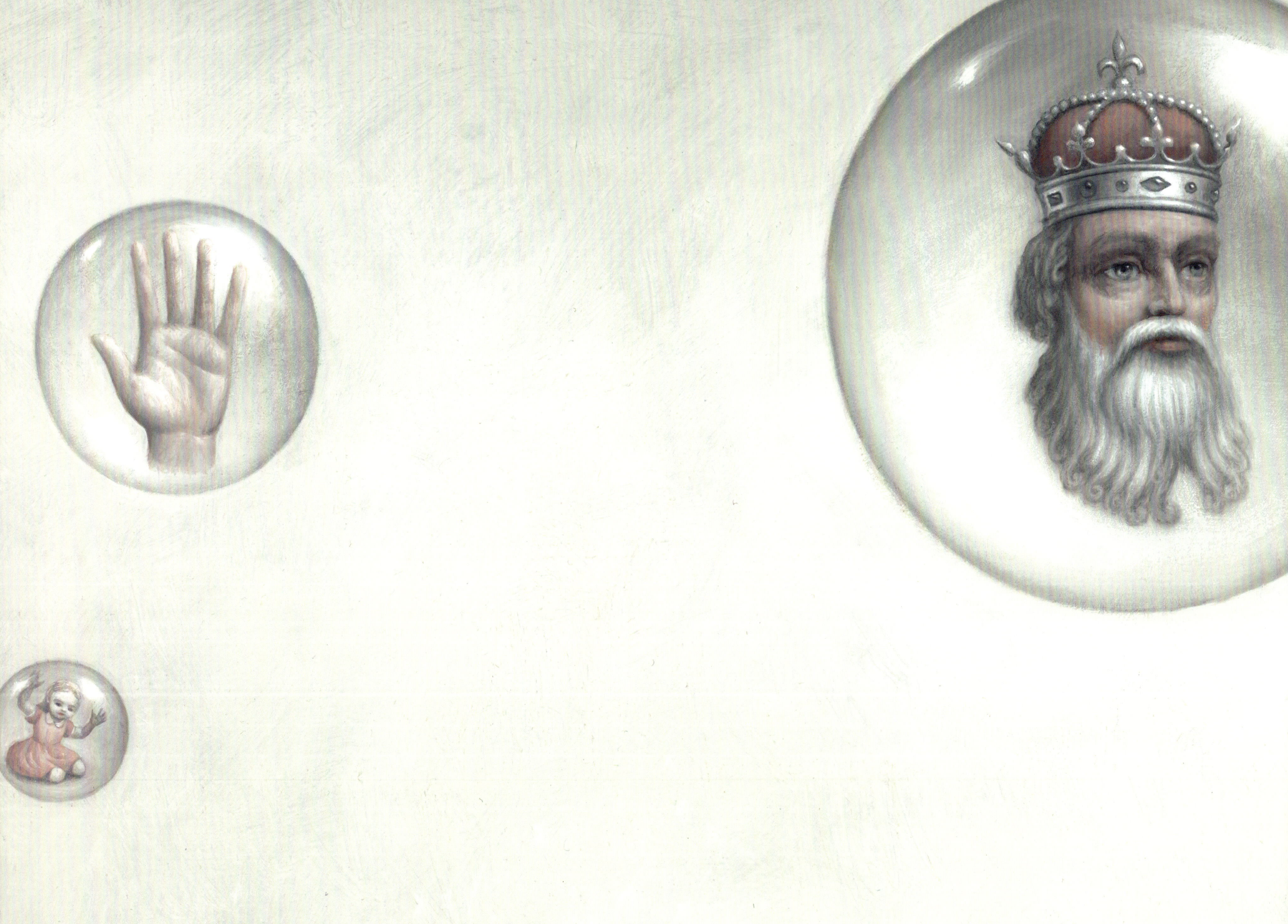

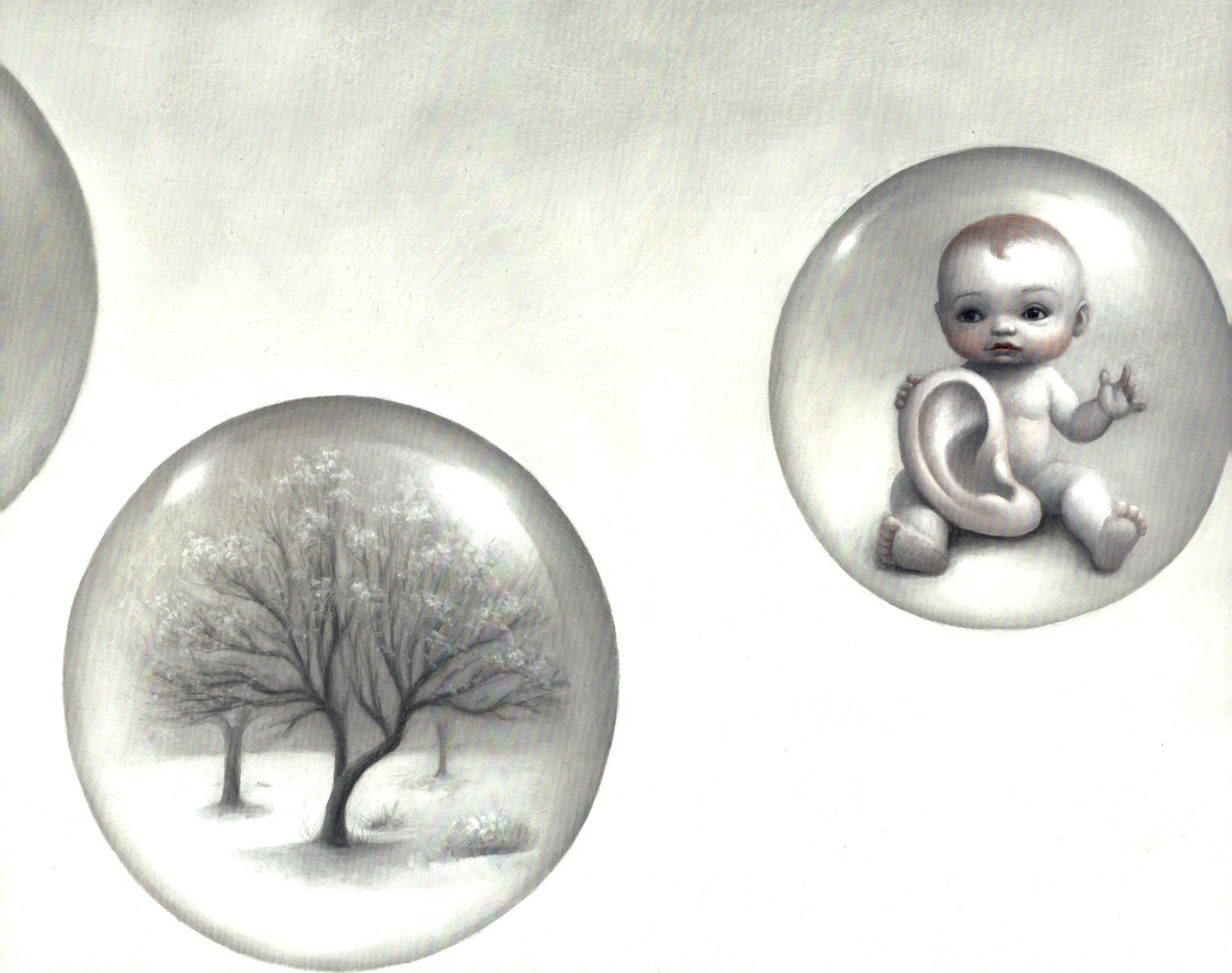

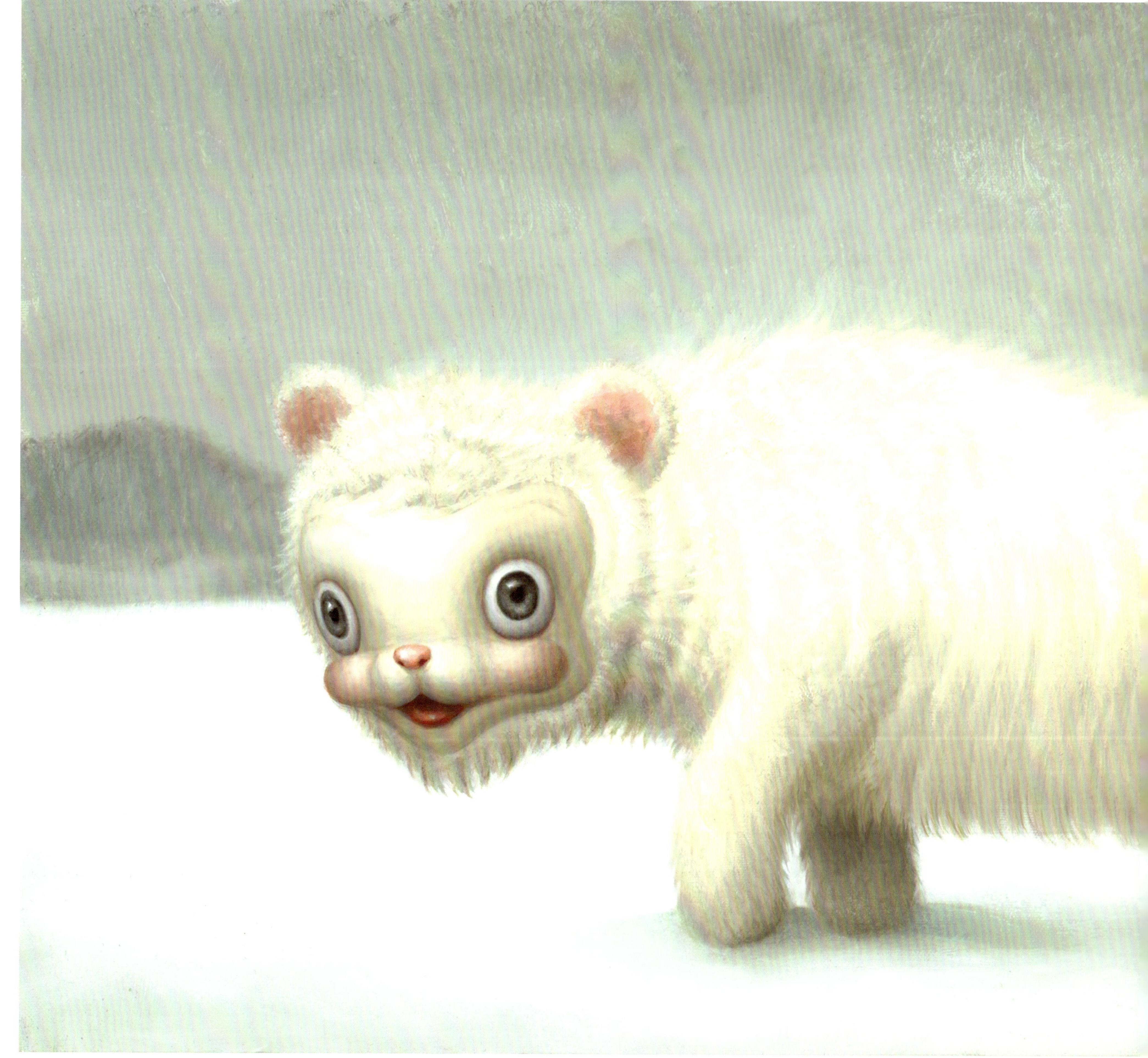

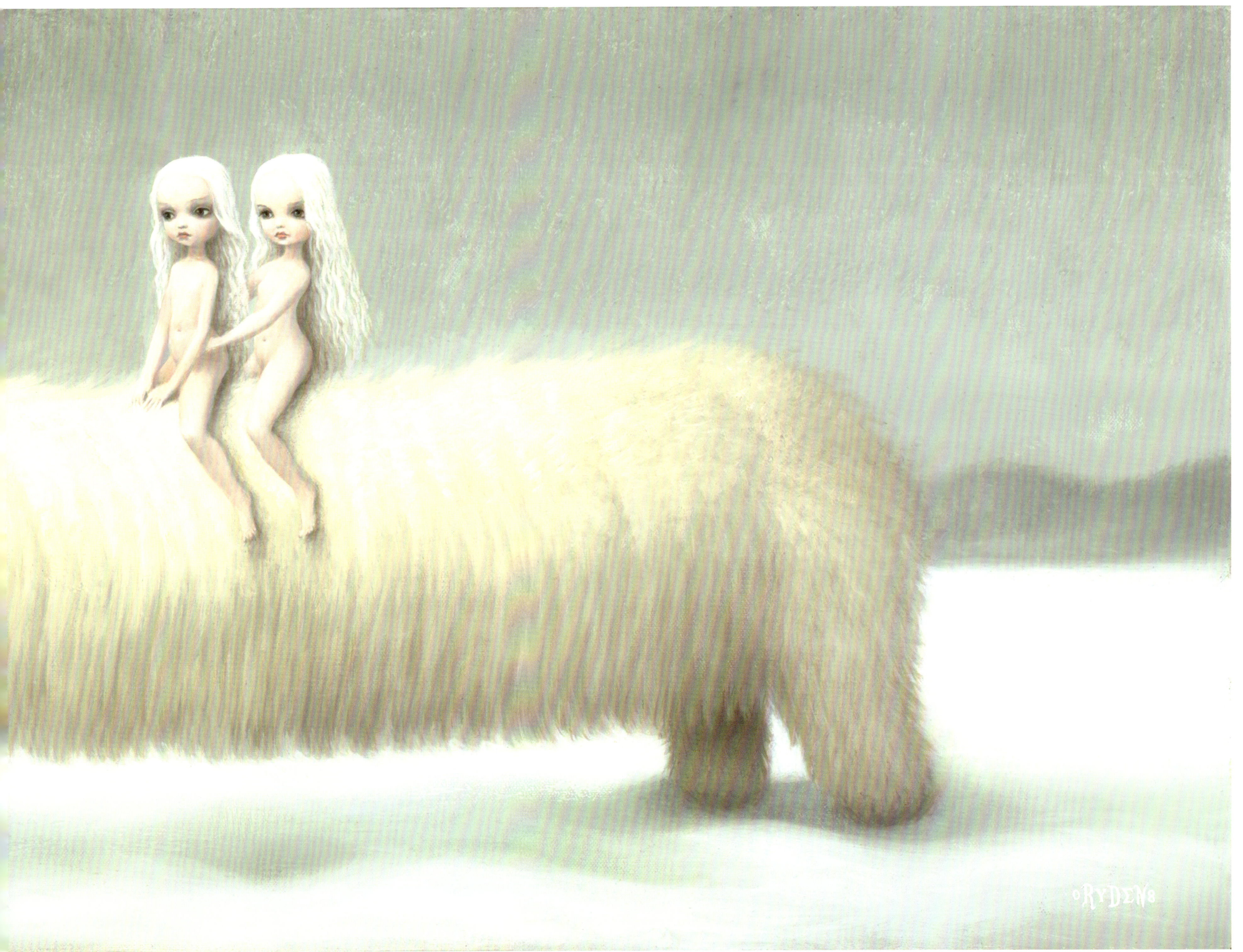

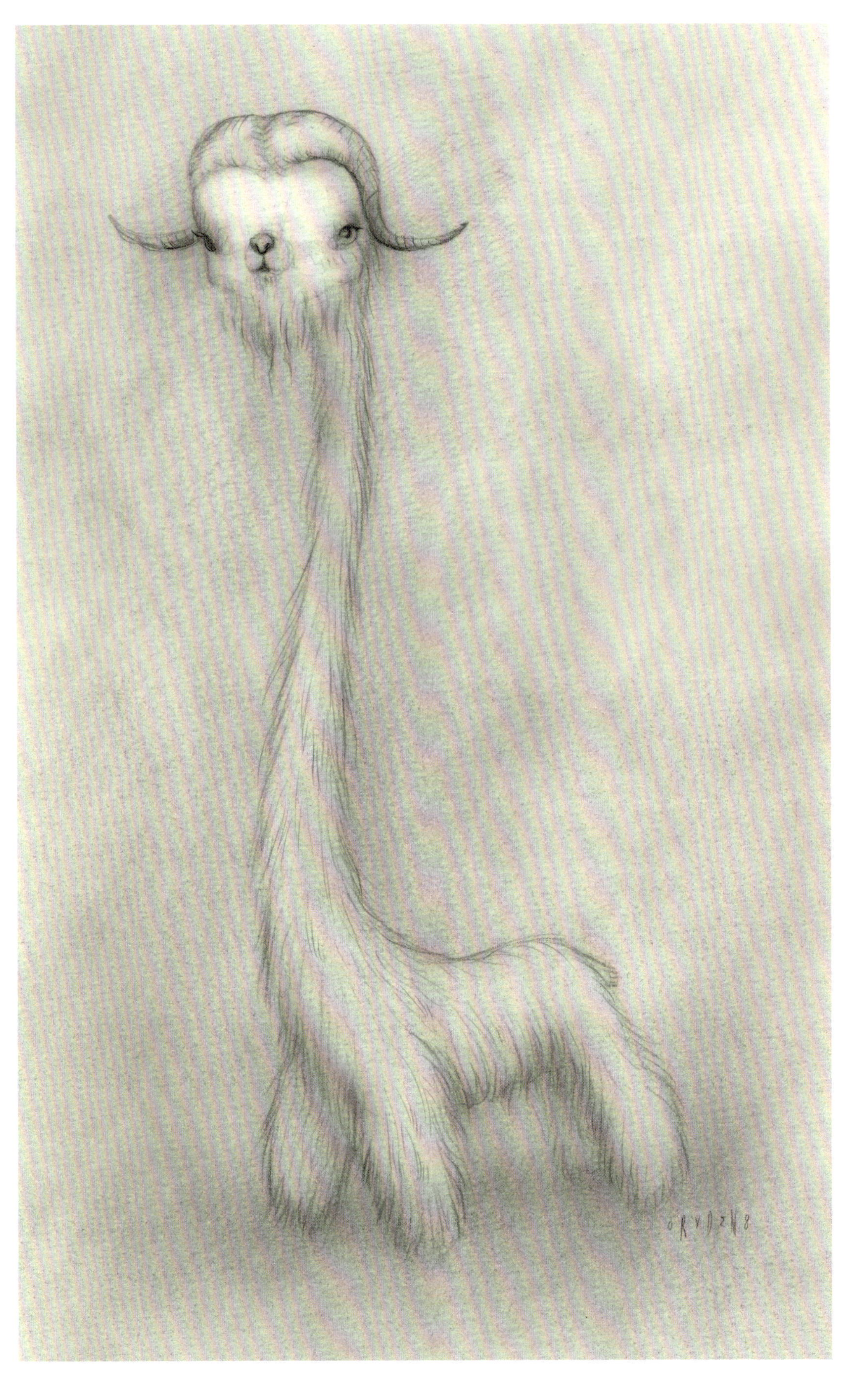

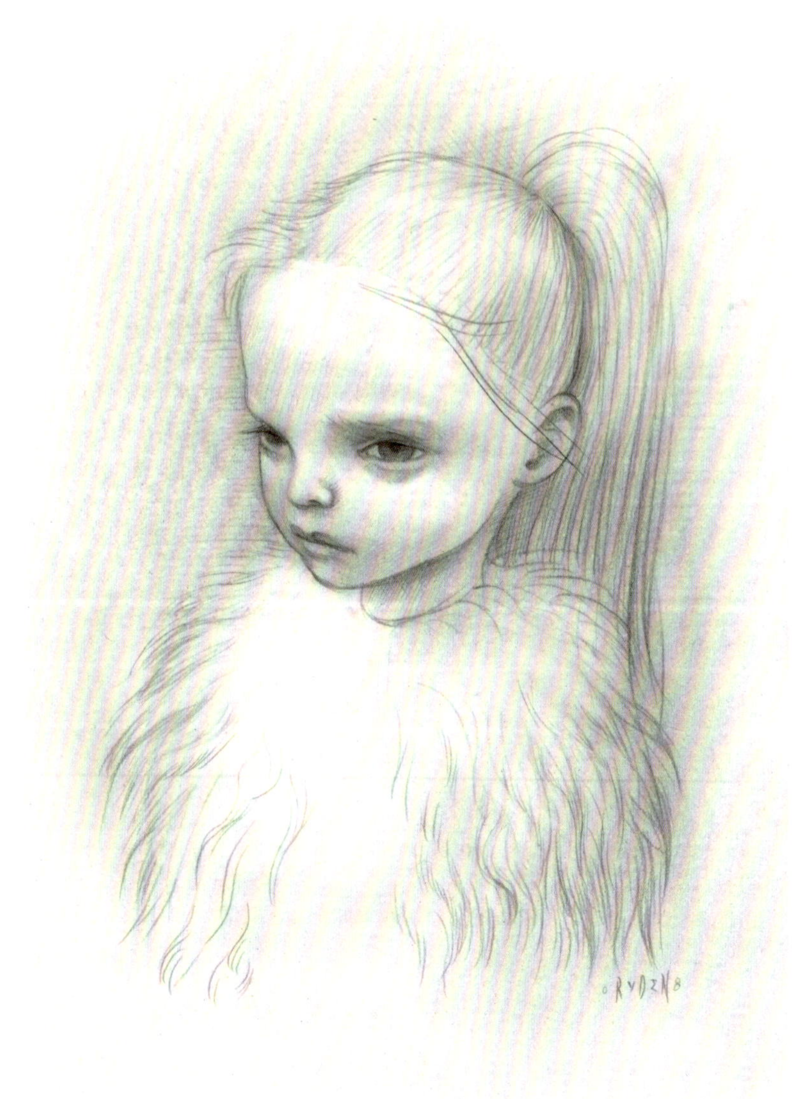

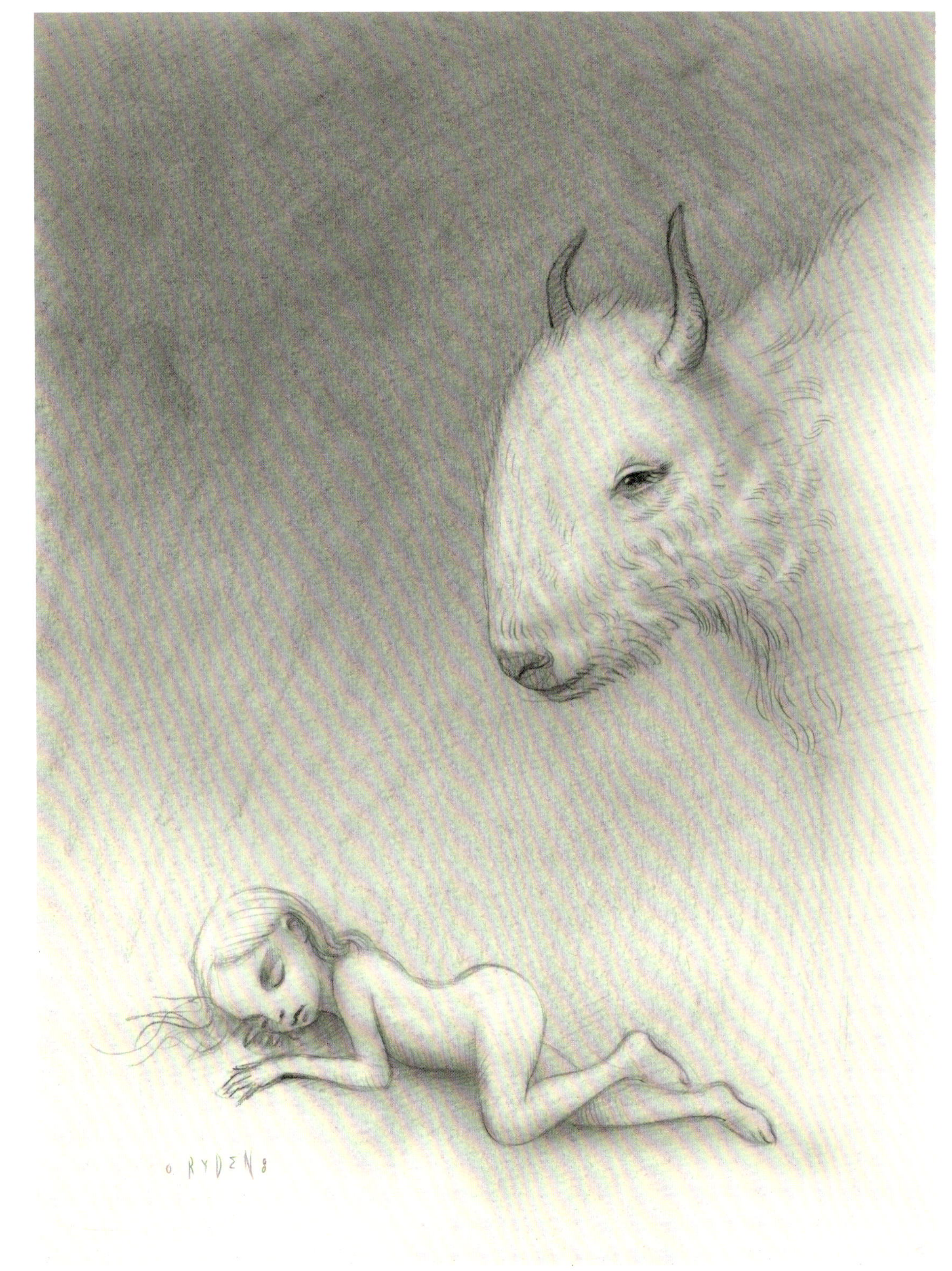

RYDEN

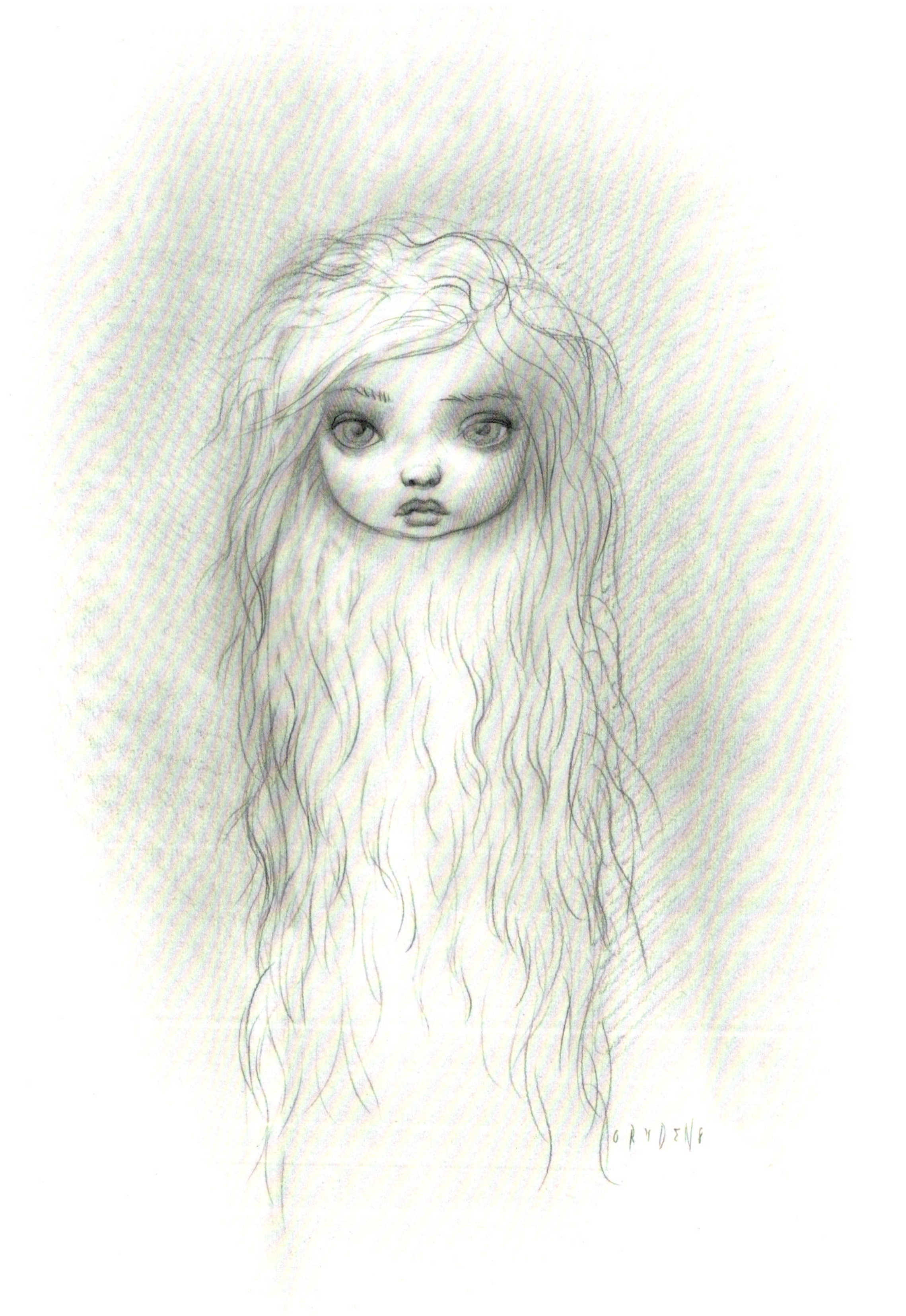

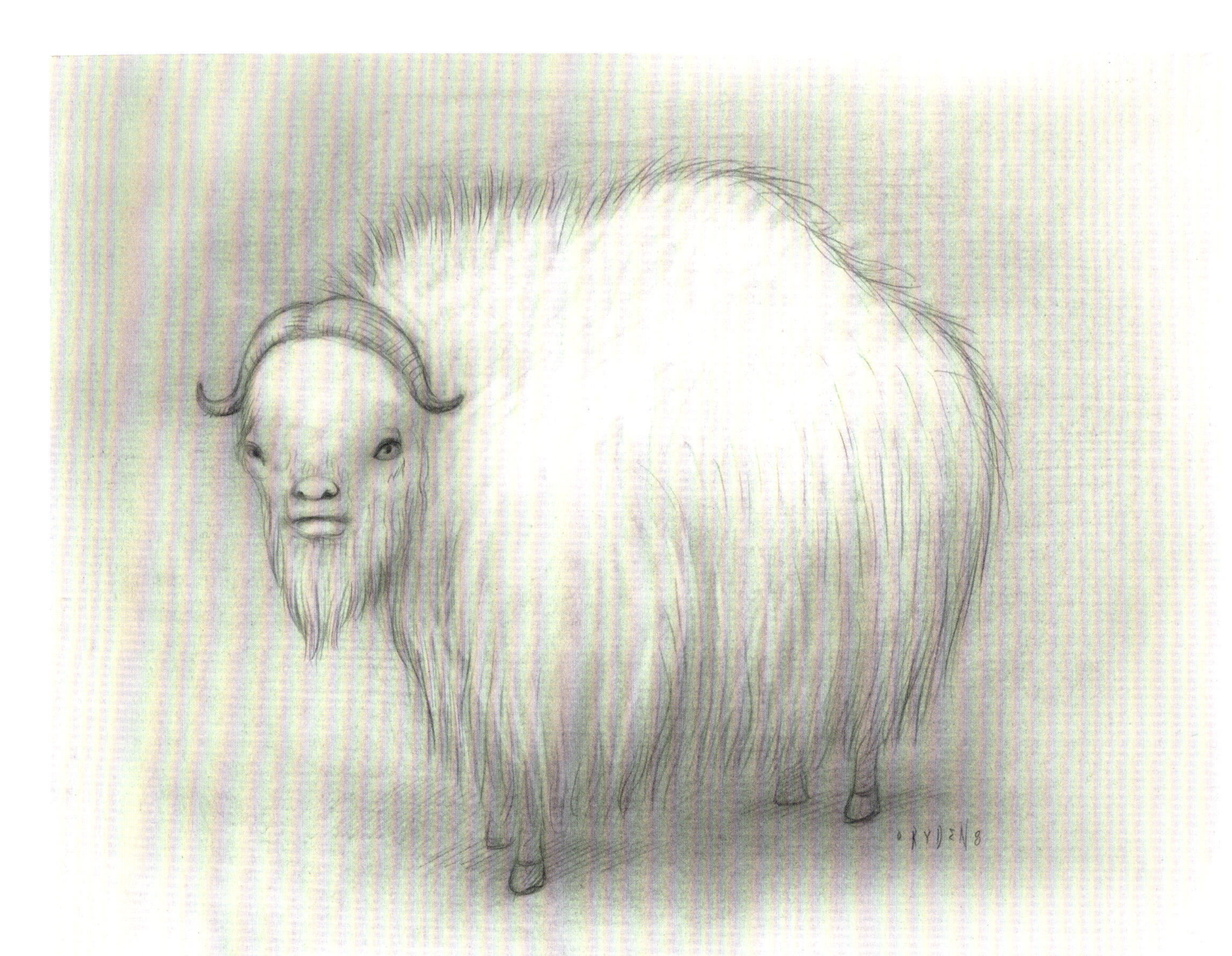

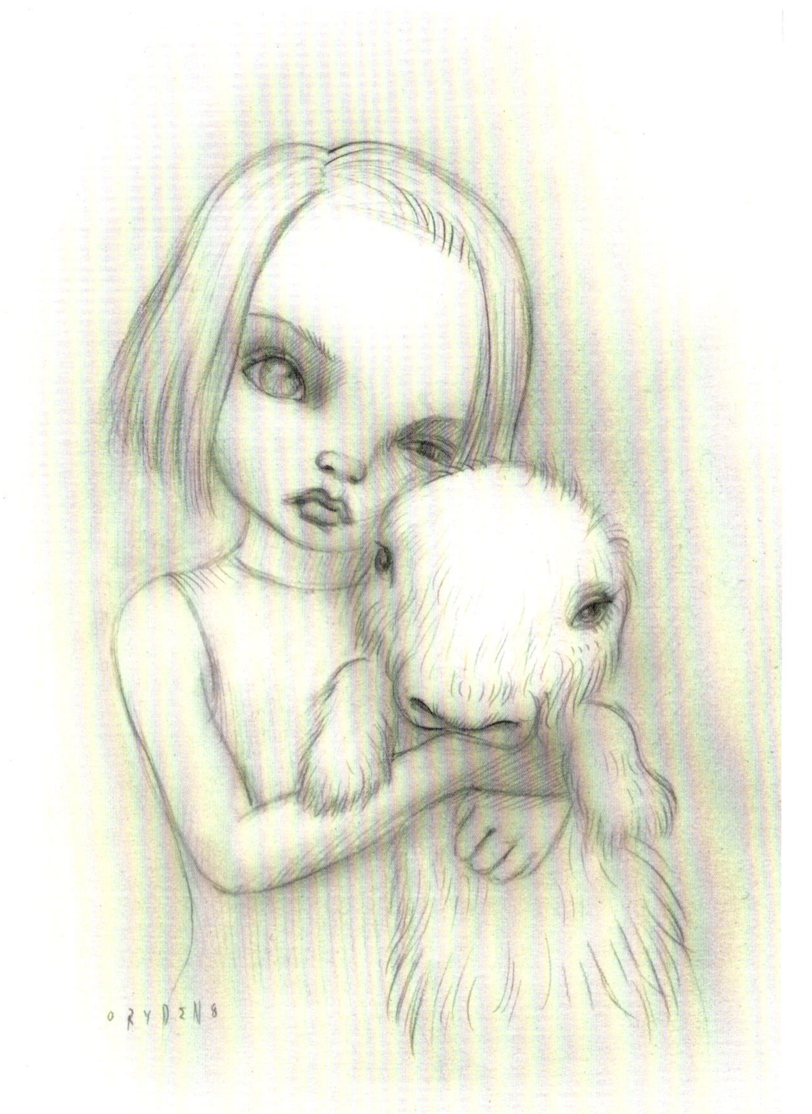

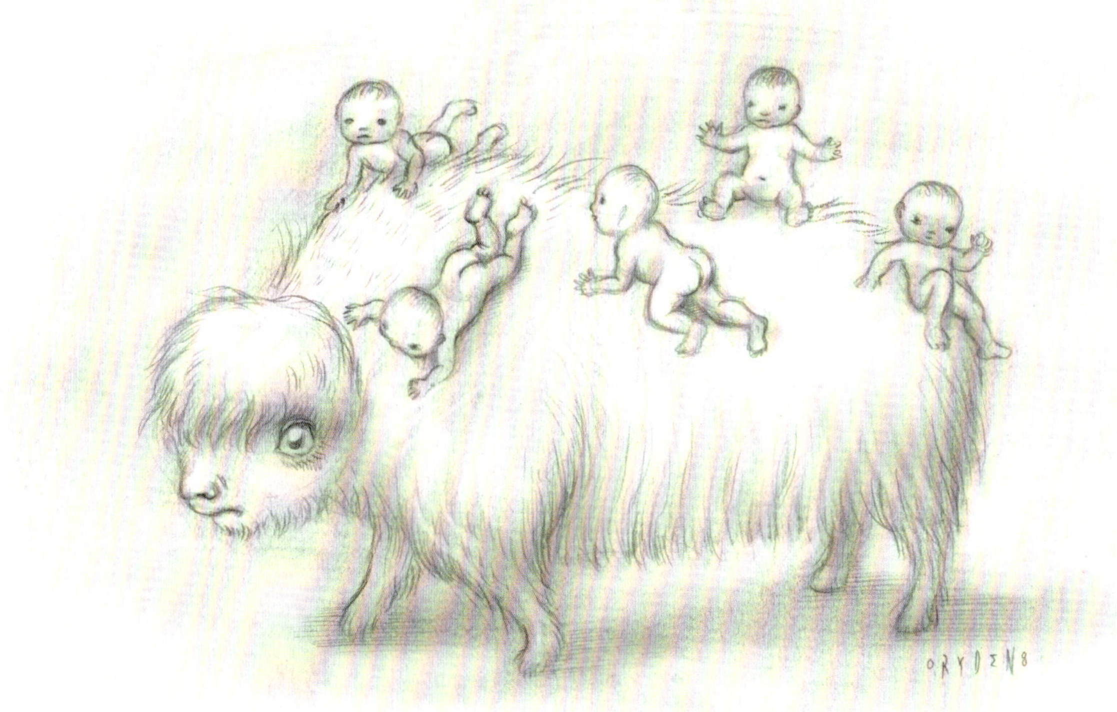

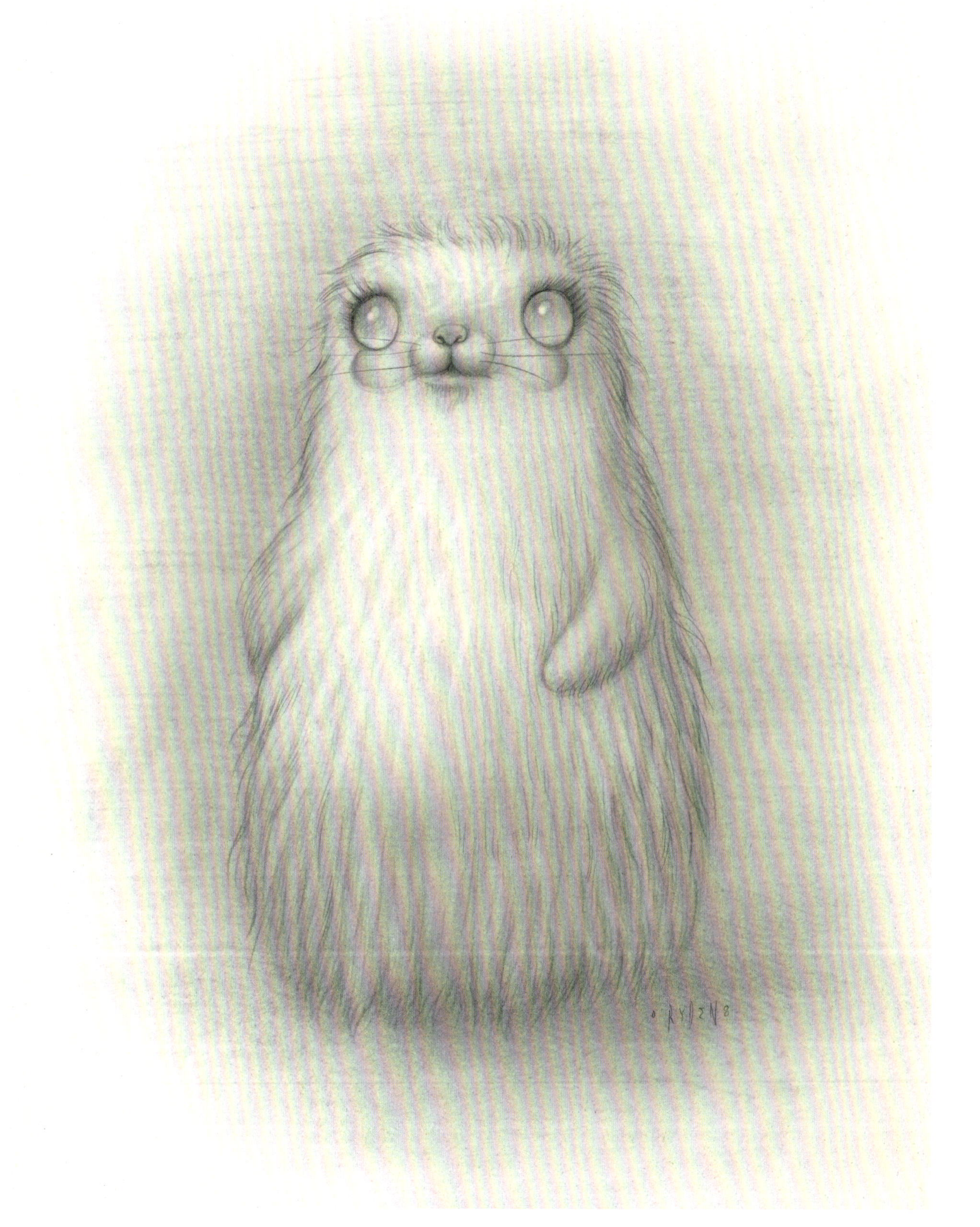

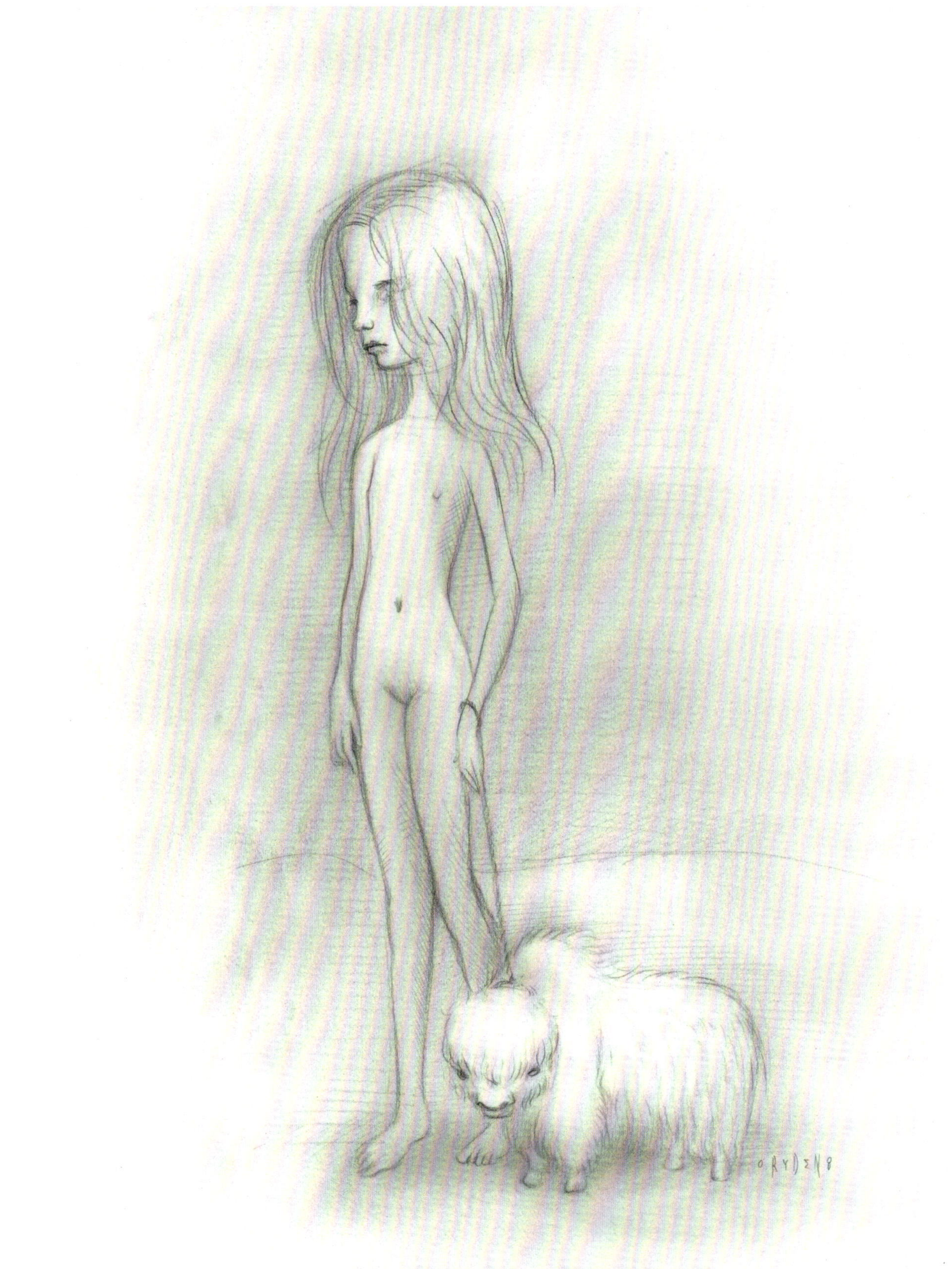

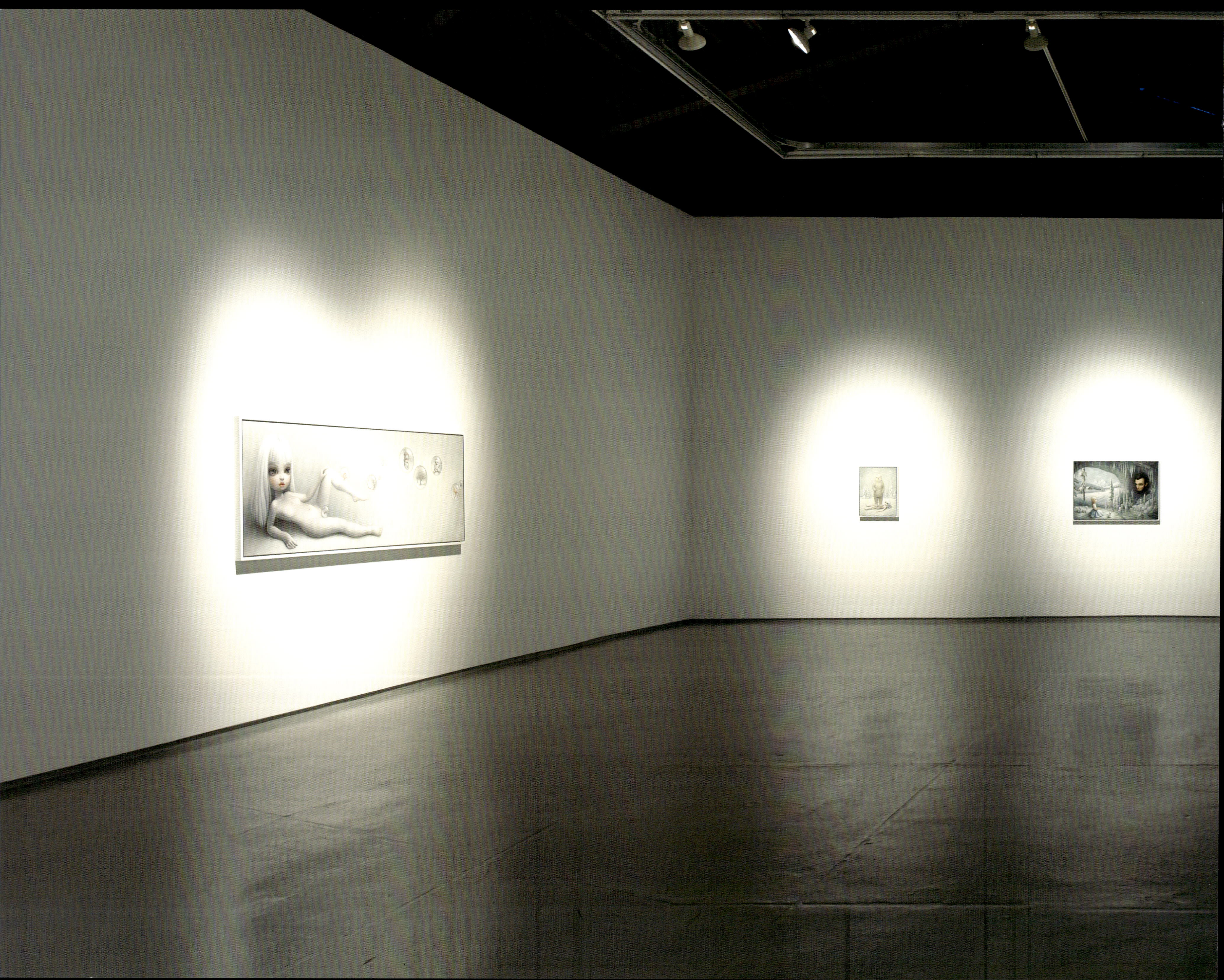

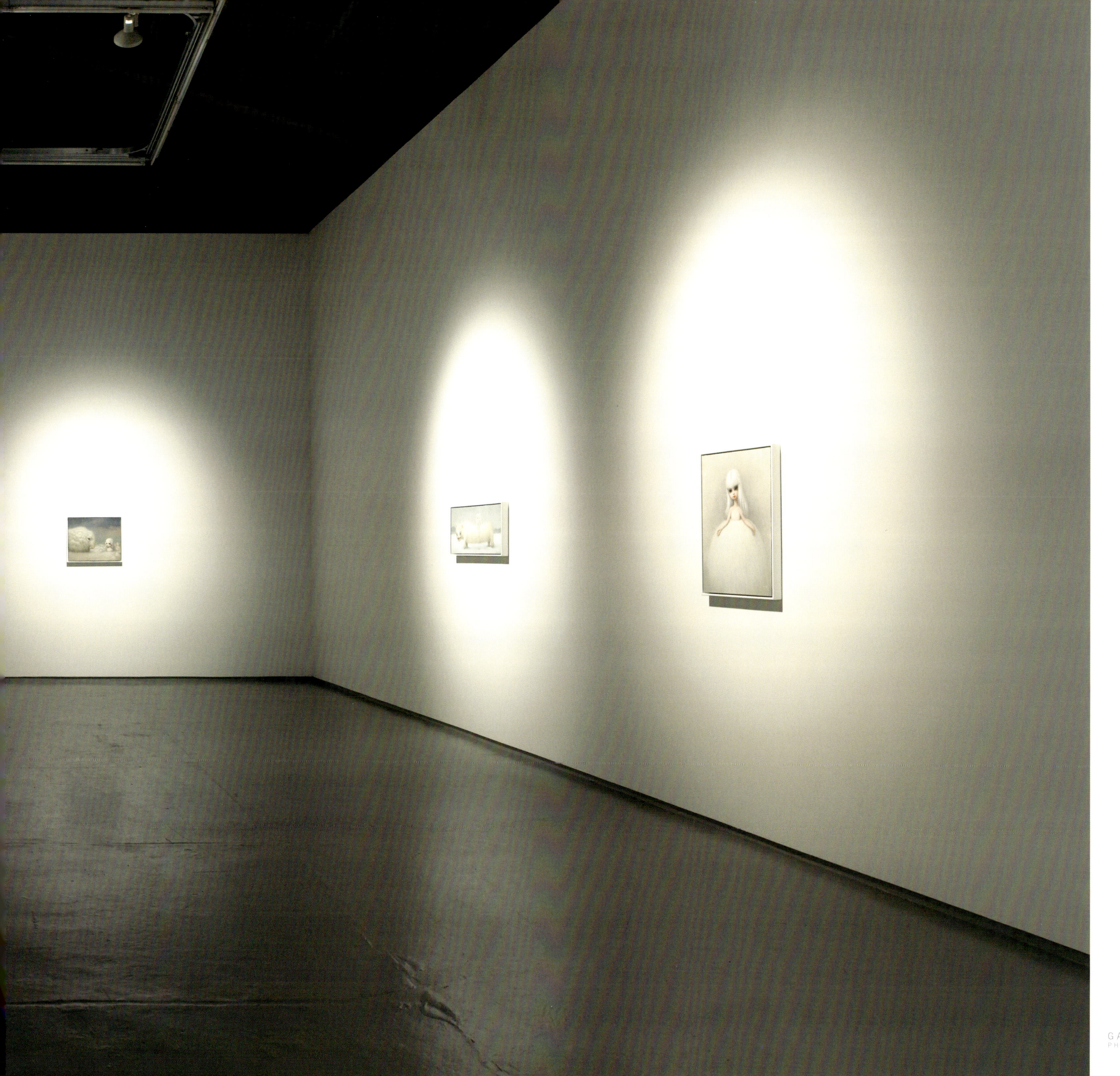

GALLERY INSTALLATION
PHOTO: KEI OKANO

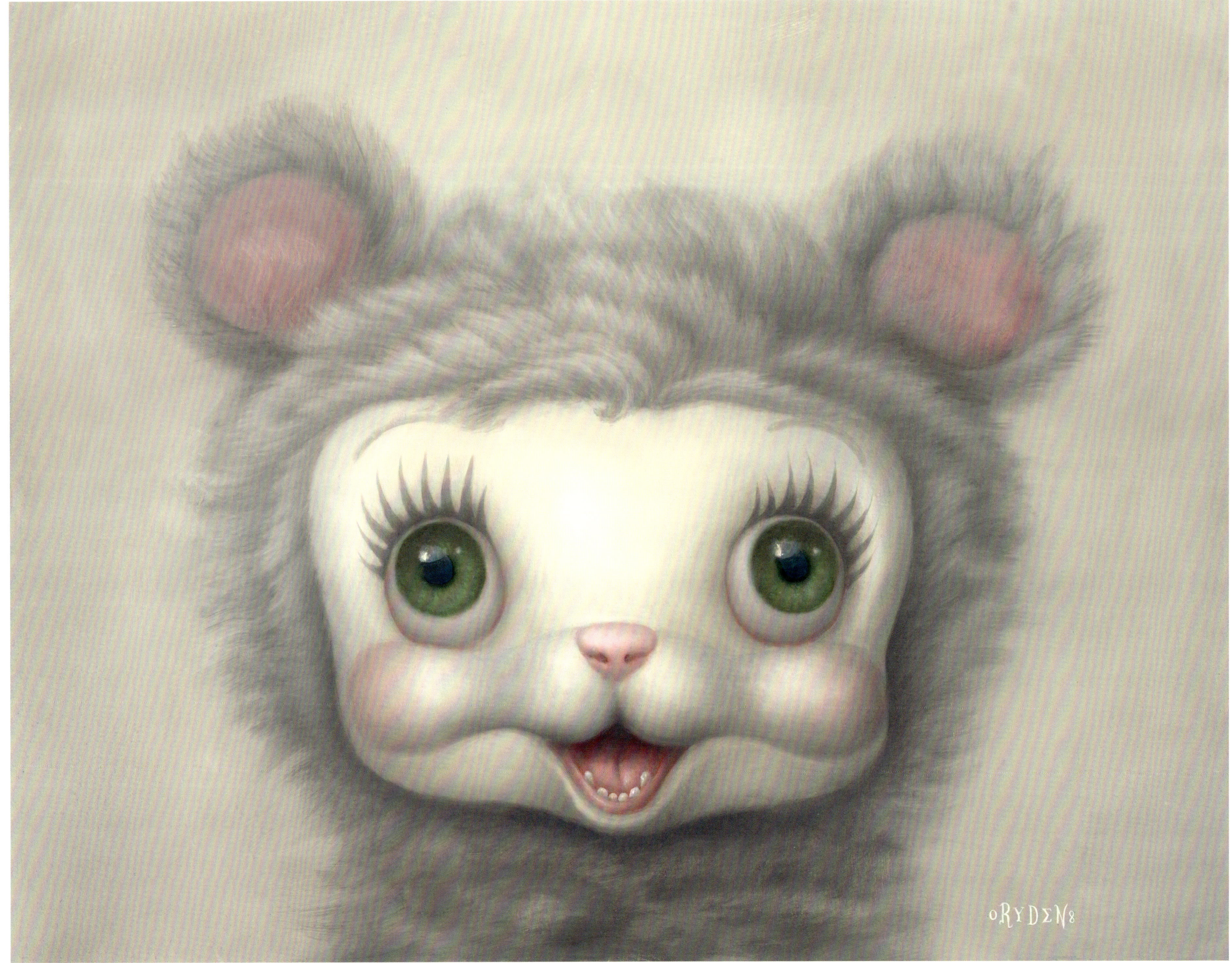

ORYDEN 8

マーク ライデン　by 奈良美智

出会い

CDショップや本屋さんって、店の前をなんか素通りできなくてついついドアを開けて中をうろうろし、結局なにかしらの獲物を手にしてレジに向かってしまう。僕とマーク ライデンとの出会いは、そんな日常の一コマの中に待っていた。今から20年近く前の話になるけど、CDショップでふと手に取ったREO Speedwagonというバンドの新譜 "The Earth, A Small Man, His Dog and a Chicken"(1990) のカヴァーの絵がなんとなくしっくりきて、けっこう長い間その絵を鑑賞していた。それでジャケ買いして店を出たのか、というとそうではなかったんだけど……とにかく単なるイラストレーションにはない作家の個性がそこにはあって、常日頃に作家の意志で描かれている中の1枚の絵だということが感じられたのだ。そして、彼の絵との次なる出会いもCDショップだった。Ringo Starrの "Time Takes Time" (1992) のカヴァーアート、そのジャクスタポッズ（並列配置）されたアメリカ西海岸風の絵に魅かれて、またまたじっくりと鑑賞してしまった……けれども、その絵でREO Speedwagonのジャケを思い出すというわけではなく、純粋にその作風を鑑賞したのだった。そして、そのCDを手に取りレジへ直行……といきたいとこだけど、Ringoは海底（Sea Deep Shop）のオクトパス・ガーデン（Octopus's Garden）のほうが居心地がよさそうだったので、また今度ということで店を出たのだった。勿体ぶってないで出会いはいつなんだよ！というと、忘れもしないそれから3年後、Red Hot Chili Peppersの新譜 "One Hot Minute" を買う！というちゃんとした目的を持ってCDショップのドアを開けたあの日、やっと自分にとって正当な形で僕はマーク ライデンと出会った。CDジャケを見てすぐにREO Speedwagonのジャケを思い出したし、音楽を聴きたいという衝動よりも、とにかく早くクレジットを見てこの絵を描いた作家の名前を知りたいと思い、僕はCDを手にすると脇目もふらずに一直線にレジへ走ったのだった。あ〜懐かしい！　その後は、ロサンジェルスに行くたびに街のギャラリーで彼の作品を探して観るのが楽しみになったのは言うまでもない。

絵画として

さて、彼の絵は90年代まではロウブローアートという括りで語られてきたように思う。事実、前出のRingo Starrのアルバムや、その前年のMichael Jacksonの "Dangerous" のジャケにも見られる色々なイメージが奇妙にジャクスタポッズされた絵が多かったし、絵画として自立させることよりも、描くことで画面上に何が出来るかということの楽しみと達成に興味を持っているように感じた。しかし、それ以後の作品に一貫しているのは、要素としての具体的モチーフを限定することによる主題の明確化と、絵画が本質的に持っている深みへの追及だ。昨今のアンダーグラウンド・カルチャーにおいて語られる、スタイリッシュに蔓延するロウブローアート、小集団意識下の大集団に属するそれらとは根本的にどこかが違う。近作に見られる説明的な背景モチーフの消失は、オーディエンスの想像力への挑戦であり、サービス精神を捨て去ることで画面本来の核であった主題を明確にさせている。そこでは画面上のメインモチーフが画家の世界を描くためだけに作動している。すなわち画家の視点がしっかりと定まっていて、構想自体が密度を持ち強く絵画化しているのだ。そしてモノトーン的に抑えた色彩では、そのグレイトーンの中に淡く見え隠れする繊細な色彩が美しく輝いている。ハイだとかロウだとか、そんなカテゴライズを曖昧にして超越する力、絵画が持っている根本的な力がそこにはある。それは同じ絵を描く者として、彼をとても羨ましく思わせる。そして、今も彼の絵をアルバムカヴァーにリクエストするミュージシャンが多く、そのために作品を提供していることも、なんか羨ましいのであった。

FINDING RYDEN

I have a hard time walking past bookstores and cd shops. I usually find myself suddenly inside them, wandering around, and eventually heading to the cash register with my prize. Mark Ryden's work was waiting for me within one such everyday event. About twenty years ago, I was standing in a cd shop with REO Speedwagon's new album The Earth, A Small Man, His Dog and a Chicken (1990) in my hands and staring long and happily at the cover. Although I overcame my desire to buy it for the cover, I felt that the image went beyond mere illustration. It looked like the work of practicing painter. My next meeting with Ryden's work was also in a cd store. It was the cover art for Ringo Starr's Time Takes Time (1992), and I was drawn to its westcoast-flavored juxtapositions. I didn't make the connection to the earlier REO Speedwagon cover, but I did spend a long time staring at the art. The tunes didn't look as friendly as Octopus's Garden, though, so I took a rain check on Ringo and left. ("Enough about you, get on with story!" you say.) Well, my first genuine encounter with Ryden's art was three years later, when I walked into a cd store to buy One Hot Minute, the new album from the Red Hot Chili Peppers, and saw the jacket. I immediately recalled the REO Speedwagon art. I wanted to get the disc right away, not so much to listen to the music as to look at the credits and find out who this artist was. I made a beeline for the cashier. What a sweet memory! Since that day, whenever I'm in L.A., I always go around the galleries looking for Mark Ryden's work.

HIS PAINTING

In the 90s, people saw Ryden's art as part of the lowbrow movement. Certainly, works like the Ringo Starr cover and the jacket for Michael Jackson's Dangerous, which came out the year before, were full of things in weird combinations, and seemed to be less about painting than about the artist's enjoyment in seeing what he could do with an image. What marks the work after this period, however, is his pursuit of painterly depth and his interest in clarifying the main subject of the image by paring down the surrounding motifs. Nowadays, all the small clusters of underground-culture aficionados, who embrace lowbrow as a style, are becoming mainstream. Ryden's work stands apart from this phenomenon. He has eliminated explanatory background motifs to put a greater demand on the imagination of the viewer, and, by abandoning the desire to please the audience, returns to his origins as painter. The main subjects in his work now serve solely to depict the painter's world. His firm, painterly approach has sharpened his eye and brought depth to his narratives. In a palette largely reduced to monotones, instances of delicate color flicker on and off in fields of grey. His work shows painting's intrinsic ability to blur and transcend all gradations of high and low. As a fellow painter, I am envious of him. I wish I had as many musicians as he still does asking me to make cover art for them.

マーク ライデンとスノーヤク　by カーステン・アンダーソン

ライデンの過去の展覧会「ブラッド(Blood)」を内なる叫び、「ザ ツリー ショー (The Tree Show)」を自然賛美と捉える
なら、最新作「ザ スノーヤク ショー」は瞑想が発露するがごときたたずまいを見せる。神秘的な銀世界に描かれたのは、
幽霊のように青白いムーンチルドレンや、奇妙だが柔らかい善意に満ちたクリーチャーたち。

今回の7つのペインティング(および数枚のドローイングとスケッチ)は、これまでの作品に比べると、祝祭的な華やかさ
は影を潜め、より静謐なものになっている。基本の色調は白だが、漂白したような白ではなく、グレーやブルー、ピンク
味を帯びた白だ。総じて構図はより偶像的で、孤独や平穏、内省を暗示する。そしていつもなら具体的な細部まで描か
れることの多い背景も、今回は整然としたモノクロームの領域へと変化している。さらに、〈アボミナブル Abominable〉
の背景にある溶けた雪片に代表されるように、過去には見られなかった抽象画の影響を感じさせる作品もある。

ドローイングの主題は少女たちと、それぞれ姿形は異なるものの、いずれも現実世界には存在しない、とはいえどこか実
在の動物に似た、精神の導き手的な存在として描かれた生き物スノーヤクだ。ドローイングはまとめて別室に展示される
形がとられたが、確かにその表現もテーマも、ペインティングとの関連性以上に、それ自体で完結している印象を与える。
ここに描かれた幼いヤクを愛しそうに抱く少女たちや、人間の赤ん坊を母親のように見守るヤクの姿には、ライデンの作
品がしばしば醸し出す不気味なユーモアは感じられない。すべての作品を支配する、アイロニーとは無縁の純粋な優しさ
は、今日ではほとんど暴力と同じ衝撃を見る者に与える。

今回、すべてのペインティングに共通する雪というテーマ。はたして展覧会の開催地が日本であることからその着想を得
たのかと問われたライデンは(なぜなら、日本の民話や神話の多くが雪のなかで繰り広げられるからだ)、ミニマリズムと
白をテーマに制作することはそれ以前から決めていたが、どちらにしてもその結びつきを喜ぶ人は多いだろうと考えたと話
した。そして、完成までに約1年を要したこのシリーズはまた、額装の簡素さにおいても際立っている。これまでライデン
がそれぞれのペインティングの延長線上にあるものとして特注で作らせてきた華美で装飾的なフレームは姿を消し、ごく
シンプルで控えめな白のフレームを使用することで、この展示の持つまばらな空間性を強調しながら、見る者がペインティ
ングそのものに集中できる余地を与えた。

マーク ライデンが今日の美術界を代表するアーティストのひとりであることは間違いない。彼の作品は、セレブリティか
ら美術館理事、ゴス系の高校生たちまで多くのファンを引き付けている。だが、この作家を興味深い存在にしている理由
は別のところにある。つまりライデンにとっては、何かを伝えることよりも、謎のままにしておくほうが重要だということ
だ。むしろ彼の場合、謎こそが伝えたいメッセージなのだと言ってもいい。錬金術や外国語、数秘学から借用したイメー
ジが散りばめられたペインティングのシンボリズムと意味について尋ねたとしても、ライデンはわざとそれを曖昧にしよう
とする。彼は謎を含んだ物語を好み、容易に解読される作品を制作するよりも、見る者に驚きと好奇心を喚起したいと
願っている。

実際、ライデンが卓越した技巧の持ち主であることに疑いの余地はないものの、人々が彼の作品に本能的に反応せざる
をえない所以は、やはりその特異なイメージと表現法にある。ライデンはその眼鏡を通して、現代的なポップの産物とSF
的驚異に、19世紀のおとぎ話と同じ種類の驚きを吹き込むことができるのだ。

批評家のなかには、ライデンの作品はただ綺麗なだけのポップカルチャーの駄作であり、視覚的なごまかしにすぎないと
切り捨てる人もいる。だが、彼が用いる一見がらくたのような現代カルチャーの断片(それを理解するか、および／または
好むかは、人によって真っ二つに分かれるところだ)の向こうには、原型的かつ神話的なイメージと、そして神秘への言及
からなる複雑なシステムが浮かび上がってくる。

実のところ、ライデンのペインティングを"理解"するには、美術史論について書かれた名著を読むより前に、ガイ・マー
チーの科学書『生物の心とからだ／生命の不思議な現象』や、ジョセフ・キャンベルの著書を読んだほうがいいぐらいだ。
もっともライデン本人は、人が彼の作品をどう解釈するかについて、きわめて禅的な許容の精神を示している。人が自分
のペインティングに異なるものを見出すことに満足を覚えるというのだ。ライデンは、どのような解釈だろうと決して同意
も否定もしない。なぜなら、大切なのは彼の作品が呼び起こす感情であって、知的な理解を得ることではないと考えてい
るからだ。

ところで、ライデン自身はこの展覧会がひとつの夢に端を発したものだと語っている。

　　〈ロング ヤク Long Yak〉で描いた長細い生き物が出てくる強烈な夢を見たんだ。夢の中で、私は1頭の
　　ヤクのお腹の中にいて、そこに開いた穴から長いヤクを眺めていた。この夢はかなり鮮明だった。
　　氷の夢は、深層心理を反映していることがある。真っ白な雪は、精神世界からきているかのようだった。

〈ロング ヤク Long Yak〉では、双子のような2人の少女が、おもちゃっぽい顔をした奇妙な獣の背に乗って雪に覆われ
た土地を行く姿が描かれる。双子はさまざまなシンボリックな意味を暗示する存在だが、彼女たちがこの生き物にまたが
る姿は、ヒンドゥー教の神々(たとえば、処女／純潔の女神として崇められるドゥルガーのような)を想起させる。こうし
た神々がトラやライオンなどの獣に乗った姿で描かれるとき、それは獣的な欲望の征服、または自我と意志の勝利を意味
する。

明らかに、ライデンのペインティングの存在理由(レゾンデートル)はその神秘性と超絶性にある。彼はまた、ミューズ
の存在についても自由に話そうとする(真夜中に彼の肩に座る"マジックモンキー"がライデンのミューズだというのは有名
な話だ)。「ザ スノーヤク ショー」の場合、ミューズは"ソフィア"という意味ありげな名を持つ白い髪の少女となって現
れる。ソフィアとはもちろん、叡智を意味する言葉であり、あるいは智慧の女神、または神の配偶者の名前としても知ら
れる。ある種の人々にとっては、ソフィアは"純潔の処女"であり、その転落が物質世界を引き起こしたのだという考えも
ある。それを考えるとき、おそらくはライデンの作品のなかでも最も挑発的なペインティングである〈ソフィアズ バブルズ
Sophia's Bubbles〉が、興味深い輝きを放ち始める。微妙な陰翳が施された抽象的な背景に横たわる、青白い肌の若い
女性。優雅で物憂げな、無垢と神聖さの両方を投影する若い女性の肖像だ。ソフィアは、彼女の性器からシャボン玉を
放射させている(いささかタイのピンポンショウのようではある)。そしてシャボン玉のなかには、太陽系のそれぞれの惑星
を象徴するシンボルがひとつずつ含まれている。つまるところ、テーマは再び人類最古の神話である万物の創造に立ち戻
ることになる。

"純潔"と"静謐"という概念は、崇高なまでに美しい〈ガール イン ア ファー スカート Girl in a Fur Skirt〉においても顕
著だ。〈ソフィアズ バブルズ Sophia's Bubbles〉と同じく、女性像のひとつの典型がそこにある。従順さと情け深さを示
す、聖母マリアのように広げられた腕と、哀愁を帯びた顔をした彼女の体は腹部まで白い毛皮のスカートで覆われている
が、胸はあらわになっている。しかし、彼女はどうやって毛皮を手に入れたのだろうか。こんな純潔の象徴のような存在
でも、ある種の犠牲を要求するものなのだ――それが、喜んで差し出されたものであろうとなかろうと。

ライデンの作品のなかで一貫して純潔の象徴として描かれる子どもたち、とりわけ少女たちは、彼らを取り巻くシュールな
狂乱と好対照をなしている。「ザ ツリー ショー」では、少女たちは森のニンフ、あるいは自然界に隠された秘密の所有者
または発見者であった。「ザ スノーヤク ショー」の場合、少女たちはさらに神聖な理想の象徴、純潔の化身であるかのよ
うだ。しかしながら、純潔は必ずしも完全な無垢を約束するものではない。なかば浮浪児のような白金髪の少女たち
は、ライデンの過去の作品の"登場人物"よりも、ずっと重い負担を背負い、より思慮深くなっているようにも見える。彼
女たちは身体性に屈することで、世俗と、しかし同時にそれよりも高みにある役割へと縛りつけられている。

〈グロット オブ ザ オールド マス Grotto of the Old Mass〉は、世界中の教会の売店などで売られている、プラスチック
製の安っぽい土産物として不滅の存在となった『ルルドの聖母』の光景を思い起こさせる。南フランスの少女が体験したと
主張した、聖母マリアが洞窟に現れ、この世の受難の到来を警告したという"真実"の物語に由来するものだ。ライデン
の作品では、第16代アメリカ合衆国大統領エイブラハム・リンカーンの幻影が聖母マリアに取り代わっている。ライデン
の偏愛の対象としてその作品中に頻出するリンカーンは、アメリカ文化においては情け深い賢者の歴史的象徴として神話
化された存在だ。だが、高邁な理想について語る際に尊敬とともに引き合いに出される一方で、そのイメージは車のセー
ルスや各種祭日用の"装飾品"にも使用される。

体から切り離された頭部のモチーフは、初期ケルト美術からオディロン・ルドンの鮮やかなパステル画まで広く見られるも
ので、いくつもの意味を内包している。〈ファー ガール Fur Girl〉では、得体の知れない存在が、ヤクのような髪を官能
的に垂らして、陰翳のある背景のなかに静かに浮かび上がっている。人形のような顔立ちと澄み切った瞳、まっすぐな視
線を持ったこの毛むくじゃらの麗人は、後光のように輝く髪に包まれている。彼女はきっと誰よりも巫女に近い存在だ。
神託をたずさえて2つの世界を行き来し、そしてその豊かな髪は、ほんの少し飼い慣らされた野生を暗示している。

おそらく、「ザ スノーヤク ショー」のなかでも明からさまな緊張感を(画面を支配する不穏さにもかかわらず)感じさせる、
数少ないペインティングのひとつが〈アボミナブル Abominable〉だ。ここでは、物憂げな表情のソフィア風のキャラク
ターの上に雪男のような生き物が仁王立ちになって、目を細めている。はたして、野蛮で予測も制御もできない自然界の
法則が、人間の啓蒙への試みを打ち砕いてしまうのだろうか？ あるいはその逆だろうか？ 実際のところ、「ザ スノーヤク
ショー」の作品にしても、これまでのすべてのライデンのペインティングにしても、人はそのシンボリズムと引用を解明す
るために何時間でも費やすことができるだろう。ここに挙げた例は単なる推測にすぎず、ライデンの謎めいた歴史的・文
化的イメージの宝庫の中味はいまだ明らかになっていない。

重要なのは、ライデンの画家としての並外れたスキルと特異なビジョン以上に、彼が夢を売る商人として成功したことだ。
ライデンは、不可知の存在を絵画という形でどこまでも表現しようとする。そして科学や宇宙の神秘を疑うことなく、同
時にそれを大いなるユーモアをもって受容するアーティストでありマジシャンなのだ。そうして彼は、無意識のうちに他者
のなかにも驚嘆のひらめきが発火することを願っている。

MARK RYDEN AND THE SNOW YAK BY KIRSTEN ANDERSON

If Ryden's previous exhibition "Blood" seemed like an inward scream, "The Tree Show" an environmental exaltation, then "The Snow Yak Show" reveals itself like a meditative exhalation. This latest body of work features an array of new scenes set in a mystical snow encrusted land populated by ghostly pale moon children and highly uncanny yet softly benevolent creatures.

In these eight paintings (accompanied by a handful of drawings and sketches), the tone is less carnivalesque and more serene than previous works. The color palette is based on whites, though hardly bleached out, richly tinged with tones of grays, blues and pinks. Generally, the compositions are more iconic, and suggestive of solitude, peacefulness and introspection. Backgrounds, normally painted in representational detail, are articulated fields of monochrome. Some of the works include previously unseen abstract painting effects (like the melted snowflake background in *Abominable*).

The drawings are of girls, and of the amorphous snow yaks that are rendered as unlikely creatures not found in the real world – more of a spiritual companion loosely resembling a real animal. These drawings were exhibited in a separate room and indeed seem to contain a whole expression and theme unto themselves, more connected to each other than the paintings. In the drawings, girls lovingly coddle baby yaks and adult yaks take maternal turns watching over human babies, all with no real hint of the morbid humor Ryden's work can often generate. An un-ironic, sincere gentleness pervades each scene, which in these days is almost as shocking as violence.

The theme of snow infuses all of the paintings. When asked if the inspiration had anything to do with the show's Japanese location (where many folktales and myths occur in the snow) Ryden says simply that he was already inspired to go the minimalist and white route but maybe thought the link was a welcome association for people anyhow. This series, which took about a year to complete, also maintains a sparseness in its framing. Rather than the over-the-top, ornate frames Ryden usually has custom carved as an extension of each painting, this show was framed in simple, unobtrusive white frames, emphasizing their sparsity but also allowing the viewer to focus more truly on the painting.

Without a doubt, Mark Ryden is one of the biggest names in contemporary art right now. His works have attracted hordes of admirers, from celebrities to museum board members to Goth high school kids. But that is not the really interesting thing about the artist. For him, the mystery is more important than the message. In fact, mystery often *is* the message. When questioned about the symbolism and meaning in his paintings, which are riddled with images taken from alchemical texts, foreign languages and numerology, Ryden remains willfully obscure. He prefers the narrative to remain cryptic, and he wants to evoke a sense of wonder and curiosity within the viewer rather than producing work that can be quickly deciphered.

And indeed, while his technical craftsmanship is beyond question, what causes people to react so viscerally to Ryden's work is his idiosyncratic imagery and the way he uses it. Through his looking glass lens the artist is able to imbue modern day pop artifacts and sci-fi marvels with the same sense of wonderment any 19th century fireside fairytale possesses.

Some critics dismiss Ryden's work as mere pop culture kitsch just painted all fancy, a visual snake oil act. However, beyond the use of modern day cultural flotsam and jetsam (which you either get or you don't, and/or like or don't) a complex system of archetypal and mythical imagery, as well as references to the arcane, emerges.

In fact, to "understand" a Ryden painting you'd do better to read Guy Murchie's *The Seven Mysteries of Life*, a science textbook, or a book by Joseph Campbell before any tome on the history of art theory. Ryden himself is very Zen-like in his acceptance of other people's interpretations of his work. He says he finds it gratifying that people can see different things in the paintings. He never seems to confirm or deny any particular interpretation because what matters most is the feeling his work evokes rather than an intellectual understanding.

Incidentally, Ryden himself says the show was inspired by a dream:

> I had an intense dream of the long creature I painted in *Long Yak*. In the dream, I was in the belly of one yak, while looking out an opening at the long yak. This dream was quite vivid. Dreams of ice can come from deep in the psyche. Clean white snow seems to come from the realm of the spirit.

In *Long Yak*, two twin-like girls ride the back of a strange toy-faced beast through a snow-covered land. Twins connote a range of symbolic meanings, while their pose on the back of this creature is reminiscent of images of Hindu deities (such as Durga, who is occasionally considered a virgin/pure goddess figure). Those deities are depicted as riding on animals, such as tigers or lions, denoting a conquering of "animalistic" desires or the mastery of the ego and willpower.

Clearly, Ryden's whole *raison d'etre* of painting is about mystery and transcendence. He speaks freely about the Muse (in his case he flippantly refers to it as a magic monkey that squats on his shoulder in the wee hours). In "The Snow Yak Show," the muse takes the shape of a young white haired girl, tellingly named "Sophia." Sophia is also the name of a universal cosmic principle, a goddess of wisdom or God's consort depending on which version you like. She appears as a "pure virgin" according to some, whose downfall led to the manifestation of the physical world. This sheds an interesting light on arguably Ryden's most provocative painting to date, *Sophia's Bubbles*. A pale young woman reclines across an abstract, highly nuanced background. This figure is an elegant and languid young female who projects the qualities of both innocence and godliness. Sophia emanates bubbles from her loins (albeit in the manner of a Thai ping-pong ball show), each of which contains a symbol representing a planet in our solar system. Ultimately, this theme harkens back to perhaps the oldest of human myths, the creation of the Universe.

This idea of "purity" and serenity is also evident in the sublimely beautiful *Girl in a Fur Skirt*. As in *Sophia's Bubbles*, it features an archetypal female figure in a classic Virgin Mary pose, with an open armed, passive and compassionate stance, a wistful countenance and clad in a white fur skirt which conceals her stomach but reveals her breasts. It is curious to wonder how the fur was acquired: Even a figure of high purity demands a certain sacrifice—offered willingly, or not.

Ryden's consistent depiction of children, predominantly girls, as virginal figures continues to act as a foil for the surrealist circus that swirls around them. In "The Tree Show," the girls are often wood nymphs, possessors or discoverers of secrets held within the natural world. In "The Snow Yak Show," they seem to be more like representations of a holier ideal, a personification of purity. However, pure does not necessarily guarantee complete innocence. These blonde, waiflike figures seem to carry a heavier burden and embody a more considered thoughtfulness than previous "characters" in Ryden's work. They succumb to the physicality that, at the same time, ties them to the world and to the role that elevates them above it.

Grotto of the Old Mass recalls a classic "Our Lady of Lourdes" scene that has been immortalized in countless pieces of plastic, kitschy souvenirs one finds in religious gift shops throughout the world. The scene commemorates the "true" story of a young girl in Southern France who claimed Mary appeared to her in a cave, and warned her of worldly hardships to come. In Ryden's version, the apparition of Abraham Lincoln replaces that of the Virgin Mary. The 16th American president (a favorite subject of the artist who appears in many of his works) has been mythologized into a historical figure of compassionate wisdom within American culture, someone who is reverentially invoked when talking about the highest of ideals and yet whose image is also used to sell cars and "tchotckes" on national holidays.

Disembodied heads recur in art from early Celtic works to the radiant pastels of Odilon Redon and they can convey an array of meanings. In *Fur Girl* the enigmatic subject appears to float tranquilly within the void of the nuanced background, sporting a luxurious fall of yak-like hair. This hirsute honey has a halo of hair that frames her doll-like face, her crystal clear eyes and her direct gaze. This figure is more like an oracle than anything else, a figure that crosses between worlds to relay information, and her wooly tresses of hair suggests a feral wildness that has been somewhat tamed.

In fact, one of the few paintings in "The Snow Yak Show" that exhibits any sort of palpable tension (despite pervasive unnerving imagery) is *Abominable*. Here, a yeti-like creature stands and squints atop another bemused Sophia-like character. Do the wild, unpredictable and uncontrollable aspects of Nature triumph over man's quest for enlightenment? Or is it the other way around? Indeed, with all the works in "The Snow Yak Show," and in all of Ryden's paintings, one could spend hours unraveling the symbolism and references. The examples provided are merely speculations rather than certain, sanctified insight into Ryden's arcane treasure trove of historical and cultural imagery.

The important thing is that beyond Ryden's formidable painting skill and singular vision is his achievement in the role of a dream merchant. He is an artist/magician who is profoundly able to express questions about the unknowable in pictorial form, and who appreciates the mysteries of science and the universal without judging it (and while having a great sense of humor about it at the same time) and unselfconsciously hoping it will ignite the spark of wonder within others.

This essay first appeared in Hi-Fructose Magazine, vol. 11

LIST OF PLATES

作品リスト

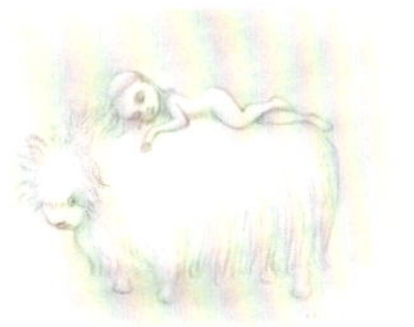

GIRL SLEEPING ON A YAK

2008

graphite on paper

26.7 x 33 cm

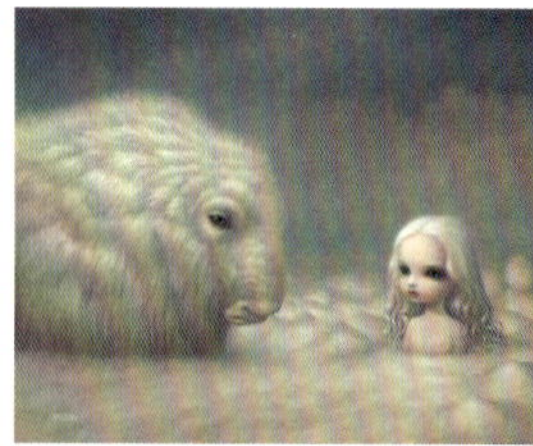

HEAVEN

2008

oil on canvas

40.7 x 50.8 cm

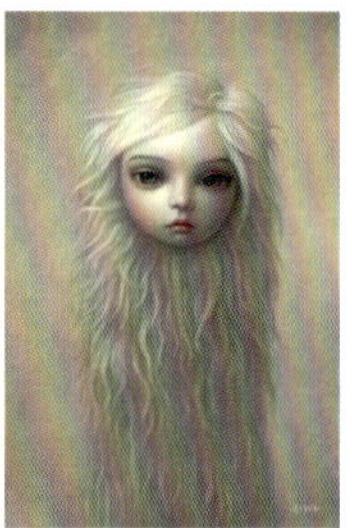

FUR GIRL

2008

oil on canvas

76.2 x 50.8 cm

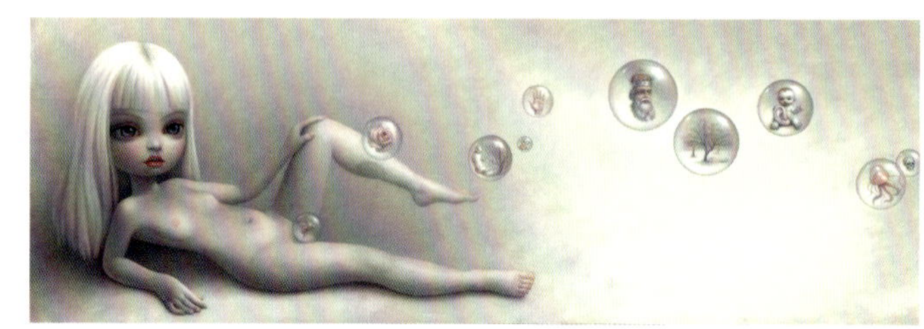

SOPHIA'S BUBBLES

2008

oil on canvas

76.2 x 228.6 cm

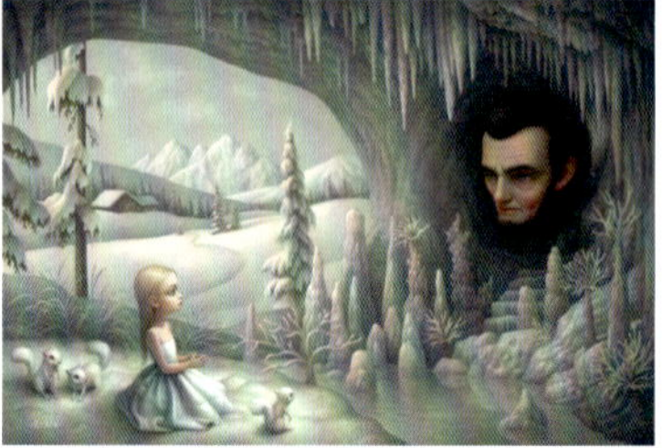

GROTTO OF THE OLD MASS

2008

oil on canvas

61 x 91.5 cm

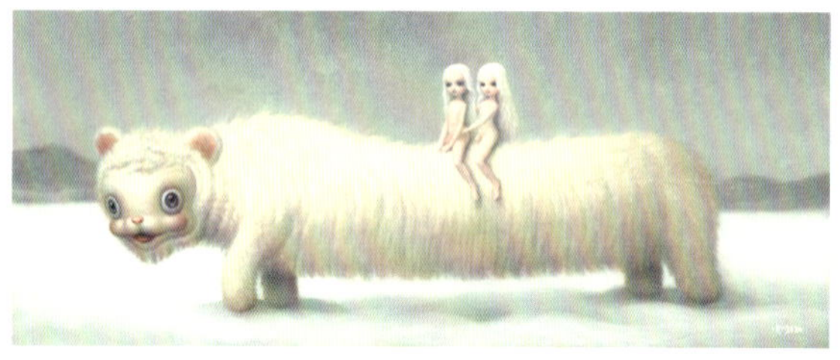

LONG YAK

2008

oil on canvas

30.5 x 76.2 cm

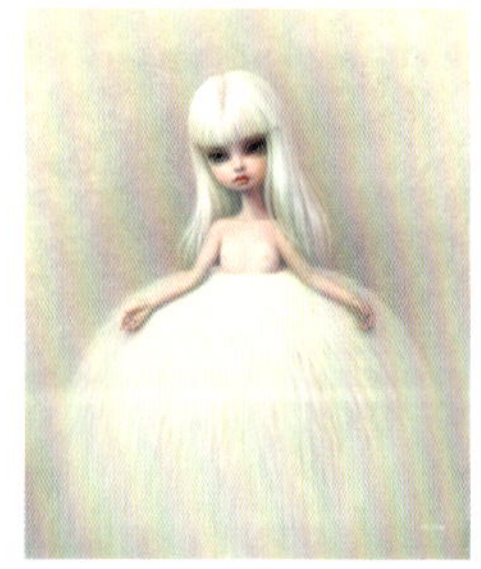

GIRL IN A FUR SKIRT

2008

oil on canvas

76.2 x 50.8 cm

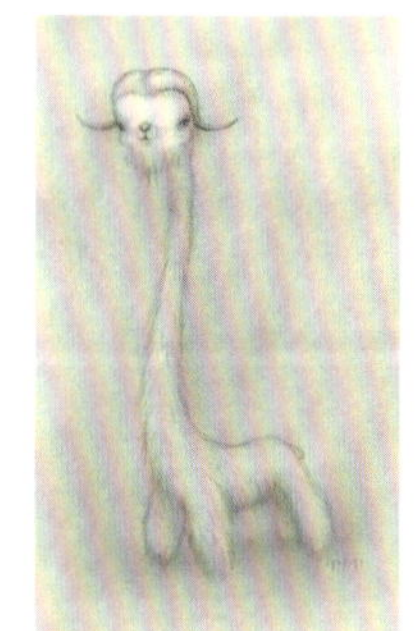

LONG NECK YAK

2008

graphite on paper

38.1 x 22.9 cm

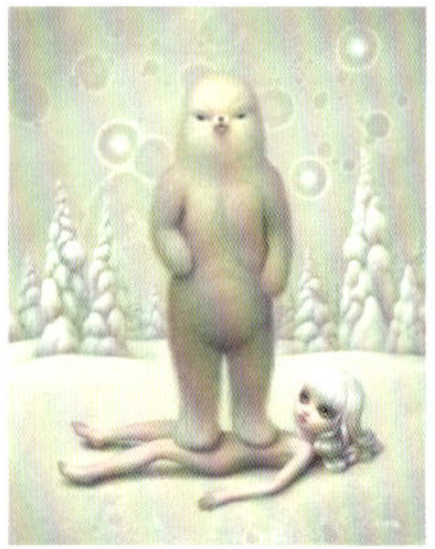

ABOMINABLE

2008

oil on canvas

50.8 x 40.7 cm

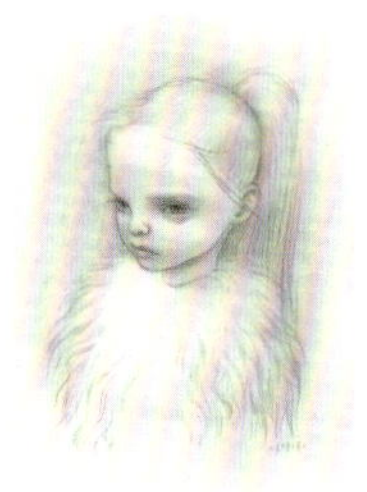

GIRL IN FUR
2008
graphite on paper
22.9 x 16.7 cm

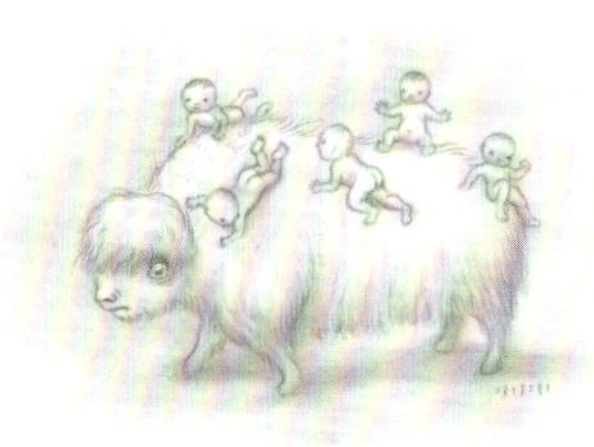

YAK WITH BABIES
2008
graphite on paper
17.8 x 25.4 cm

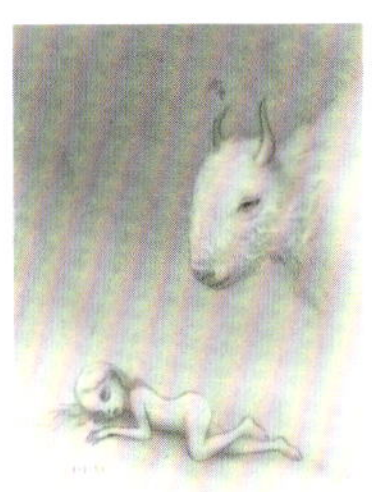

YAK DREAM
2008
graphite on paper
24 x 31.8 cm

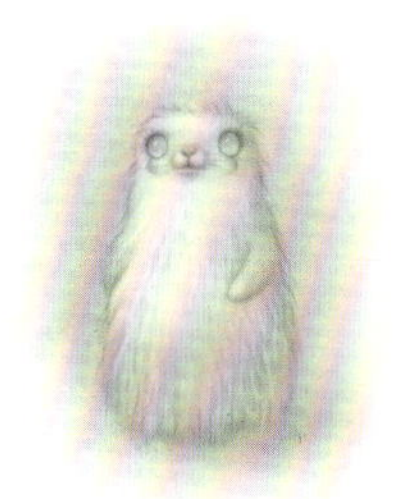

YOUNG YAK
2008
graphite on paper
34.3 x 26.7 cm

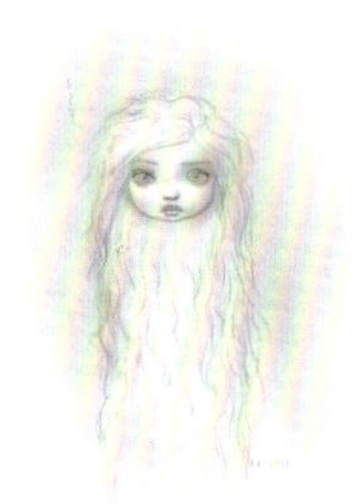

FUR GIRL DRAWING
2008
graphite on paper
35.6 x 22.9 cm

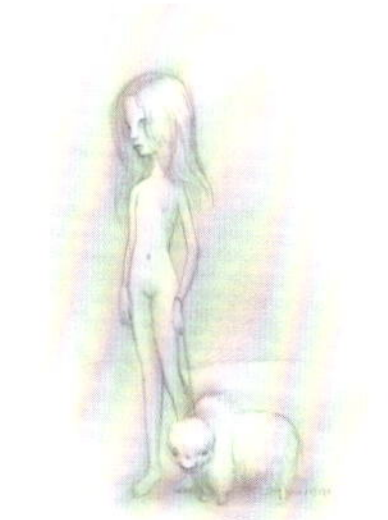

PET YAK WALK
2008
graphite on paper
35.6 x 25.4 cm

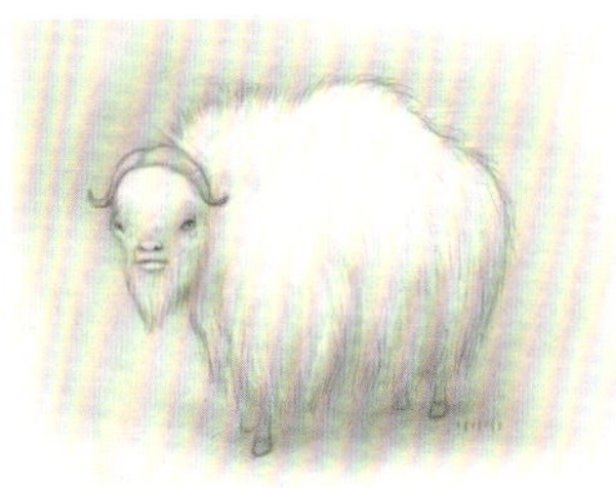

OLD YAK
2008
graphite on paper
22.9 x 30.5 cm

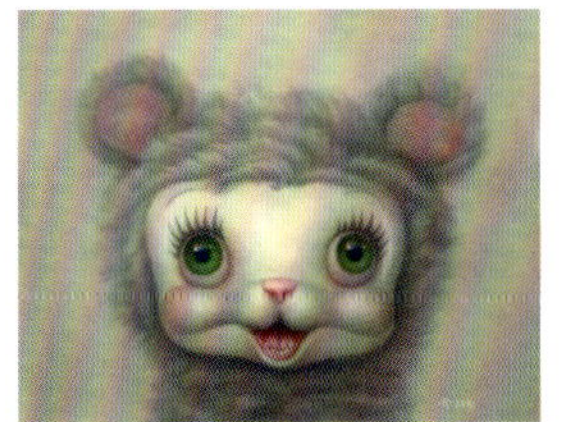

SNOW YAK
2008
oil on panel
28 x 38.1 cm

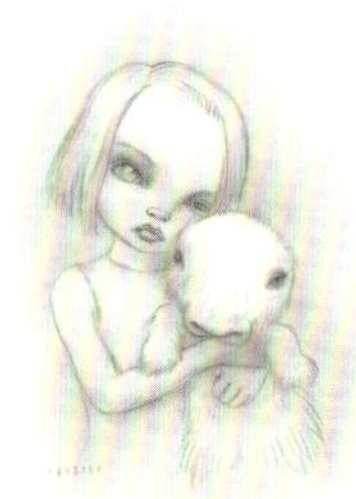

PET YAK HUG
2008
graphite on paper
22.9 x 17.8 cm

MARK RYDEN

b. 1963 Medford, Oregon
Lives and works in Los Angeles, California

BFA   Art Center College of Design, 1987

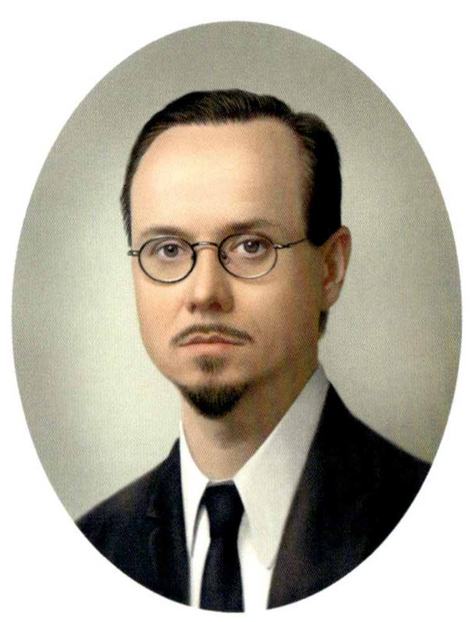

マーク ライデン

1963年
米国オレゴン州 メドフォード生まれ。
カリフォルニア州 ロサンジェルス在住。

1987年
アート・センター・カレッジ・オブ・デザインにて
BFA (Bachelor of Fine Arts ／美術学士)取得。

SELECTED SOLO EXHIBITIONS

主な個展

2010
"The Gay 90's – Olde Tyme Art Show," Paul Kasmin Gallery, New York, New York

2009
"The Snow Yak Show," Tomio Koyama Gallery, Tokyo, Japan

2007
"The Tree Show," Michael Kohn Gallery, Los Angeles, California

2005
"Wondertoonel," Pasadena Museum of California Art, Pasadena, California

2004
"Wondertoonel," Frye Art Museum, Seattle, Washington

2003
"Blood," Earl McGrath Gallery, Los Angeles, California
"Insalata Mista," Mondo Bizarro Gallery, Bologna, Italy

2002
"Bunnies and Bees," Grand Central Art Center, Santa Ana, California

2001
"Bunnies and Bees," Earl McGrath Gallery, New York, New York
"Amalgamation," Outré Gallery, Melbourne, Australia

1998
"The Meat Show," Mendenhall Gallery, Pasadena, California

SELECTED GROUP EXHIBITIONS

主なグループ展

2009
"Pictopia—Festival of New Character Worlds," Haus der Kulturen der Welt, Berlin, Germany

2008
"Prints from the Cal State Fullerton University Collection II", Cal State Fullerton Main Art Gallery, Fullerton, CA
"In the Land of Retinal Delights," Laguna Art Museum, Laguna Beach, California

2007
"El rey de la casa," Institut de Cultura de Barcelona, Spain

2006
"Drawn to Expression," Art Center College of Design, Pasadena, California

2005
"Au Pays de Merveilles," Galerie Magda Danysz, Paris, France

2004
"Innocence Found," DFN Gallery, New York, New York
"100 Artists See Satan," Grand Central Art Center, Santa Ana, California
"Juxtapoz 10th Anniversary Group Show," 111 Minna Gallery, San Francisco, California

2003
"Dark Fairytales," Roq La Rue Gallery, Seattle, Washington
"Group Show," La Luz De Jesus Gallery, Los Angeles, California
"Raising the Brow," Earl McGrath Gallery, Los Angeles, California

2002
"Hello," PressPop Gallery, Tokyo, Japan
"Gods and Monsters," Roq La Rue Gallery, Seattle, Washington
"Group Show," La Luz De Jesus Gallery, Los Angeles, California
"Draw," Roq La Rue Gallery, Seattle, Washington
"Von Dutch an American Original," Northridge Art Galleries, Northridge, California

2001
"Representing LA, Pictorial Currents in Southern CA Arts," Frye Art Museum, Seattle, Washington
"Representing LA, Pictorial Currents in Southern CA Arts," Laguna Art Museum, Laguna Beach, California
"Group Show," La Luz De Jesus Gallery, Los Angeles, California

2000
"Margaret Keane and Keaneabilia," Laguna Art Museum, Laguna Beach, California
"Luck of the Draw," La Luz De Jesus Gallery, Los Angeles, California
"Up From the Underground," Hollywood Arts & Culture Center, Hollywood, Florida

1999
"Group Show," Copro-Nason Gallery, Culver City, California
"Six Forms of Love and Despair," Merry Karnowsky Gallery, Los Angeles, California
"Invitational II," La Luz De Jesus Gallery, Los Angeles, California

1998
"Kittens'n'Kads," Merry Karnowsky Gallery, Los Angeles, California
"Tribute to La Luz de Jesus," Track 16 Gallery, Los Angeles, California

1997
"Calivera Kustom," Merry Karnowsky Gallery, Los Angeles, California

1996
"21st Century Tiki," La Luz De Jesus Gallery, Los Angeles, California

1994
"Side Show," Tamara Bane Gallery, Los Angeles, California

SELECTED BIBLIOGRAPHY

主な文献目録

"The Gay 90s: Old Tyme Art Show"
by Ken Johnson
New York Times (May 2010)

"(My Inspiration is…) Mark Ryden"
Vogue Nippon (May 2009)

"Mark Ryden"
by Sakiko Fukuhara
Dazed & Confused Japan (April 2009)

マーク・ライデンの毛ものっ娘
Geijutsu Shincho (April 2009)

マーク・ライデン展「ザ・スノーヤク・ショー」
SO-EN (March 2009)

"Mark Ryden and the Snow Yak"
by Kirsten Anderson
Hi-Fructose (March 2009)

"Snow Yaks and Yetis – An Ice Man Cometh"
by Manami Okazaki
Japan Times (February 2009)

"Pageant of the New Old Masters"
by Theo Douglas
District (July 2008)

"Living the Dream"
by Teena Apeles
Helio (Fall 2007)

"Natural Mystic"
by Steven Psyllos
Trace (May 2007)

"Mark Ryden's Tree Show
Embraces His Golden Bear"
by Michael Cervin
Juxtapoz (May 2007)

"Shooting Low, Aiming High"
by Holly Myers
LA Weekly (March 22, 2007)

"The Forest for the Trees"
by Michael Cervin
Los Angeles CityBeat (March 15, 2007)

"Surreal Visual Art"
by Lulu Tzeng
DPI (February 2007)

"Pop Surrealismo"
by David Vecchiato
La Republica XL (September 2006)

"Mark Ryden"
Art Prostitute (2006)

"Ring Around the Rosie"
by Attaboy and Annie Owens
Hi-Fructose (July 2006)

"Il Volto Pop del Surrealizmo"
by Luca Beartrice
Arte (March 2006)

Artist Feature
Parteaguas (Spring 2006)

"Mark Ryden"
by Elsa Garcia
Umbigo (2006)

Artist Feature
by M. Marisa Luiso
.ISM (Winter 2005)

"Pictures from the Unibrow Revolution"
by Doug Harvey
LA Weekly (October 17, 2005)

"Angel/Demon"
by Jose Carlos Suarez
The Creator Studio (October 2005)

Artist Feature
by Eva Roy
Pacha Madrid (September 2005)

Artist Feature
H (September 2005)

"Welcome to Mark Ryden's Wondertoonel"
by Katrina Kaufman
Venice (April 2005)

"Wondertoonel: Paintings by Mark Ryden"
Juxtapoz (March/April 2005)

"The Ryden on the Wall"
by Evan Nicoll-Johnson
Flaunt (February 2005)

Artist Feature
id Pure (2005)

Artist Feature
by Ekin Sanac
Bant (2005)

"Mark Ryden's Blood Show"
by Elodie Denis
Versus (January/February 2004)

"Blood: Miniature Paintings of
Sorrow and Fear"
by Chuck Amok
Juxtapoz (September/October 2003)

"Mark Ryden Blood: Miniature
Paintings of Sorrow and Fear"
by Simon Hebert
Contemporary (May 2003)

"Le Cabinet du Dr. Ryden"
by Stèphanie Hervè
Elegy (April/May 2002)

"Art; Creepy, Comic, and
Very Bloody Visions"
by Leah Ollman
Los Angeles Times (April 4, 2003)

"Distress Signals"
by Doug Harvey
LA Weekly (April 17, 2003)

"Mark Ryden – The Alchemist's Message"
by Carlo McCormick
Juxtapoz (January/February 2002)

"I See Lowbrow People"
by Doug Harvey
LA Weekly (January 9, 2002)

"Late-Night Inspiration in Knickknacks"
by Vivian Letran
Los Angeles Times (January 4, 2002)

"Mark Ryden's Pop Alchemy"
by Gloria Bazocchi
Cyberzone (2002)

"Mark Ryden"
by Lily Faust
New York Art World (December 2001)

"Mark Ryden – Bunnies and Bees"
by Grace Glueck
New York Times (November 7, 2001)

"Monkey Magic"
by Sophie Pike
Oyster (October/November 2001)

"Meat Glorious Meat"
by Glenn Peters
Black+White (October 2001)

"Mark Ryden: The Golden Child"
by Duda Fernandez
Tear (September 2001)

"The Meat Alchemist"
by Noko
P.U.R.E. (2001)

"Overacheiver Extraordinaire"
by Long Gone John
Juxtapoz (Winter 1998)

"Carnivour's Delight"
by Rick Gilbert
Panik Magazine (November 1998)

Artist Feature
by Hope Urban
Juxtapoz (Spring 1995)

SELECTED PUBLICATIONS

主な出版物

2010
Speak for the Trees
by Andria Friesen
Friesen Gallery
Seattle, Washington

2009
Pictopia
Kirsten Einfeldt
Haus der Kulturen der Welt
Berlin, Germany

2008
The Upset – Young Contemporary Art
Robert Klanten, Pedro Alonzo
Die Gestalten Verlag GmbH & Co.
Berlin, Germany

2006
Fushigi Circus
Essay by Nagi Noda
PIE Books
Tokyo, Japan

Wondertoonel
Exhibition Book
Essay by Debra Byrne
Frye Art Museum
Seattle, Washington

2005
LA Artland
by Chris Kraus, Jan Tumlir
and Jane McFadden
Black Dog Publishing
Los Angeles, California

2004
Pop Surrealism
Edited by Kirsten Anderson
Last Gasp
San Francisco, California

2003
Blood
Exhibition Book
Porterhouse Fine Art Editions
Los Angeles, California

2001
Bunnies and Bees
Exhibition Book
Essay by Mike McGee
Porterhouse Fine Art Editions
Los Angeles, California

2001
Anima Mundi
Essay by Carlo McCormick
Last Gasp
San Francisco, California

1998
The Meat Show
Exhibition Book
The Mendenhall Gallery
Pasadena, California

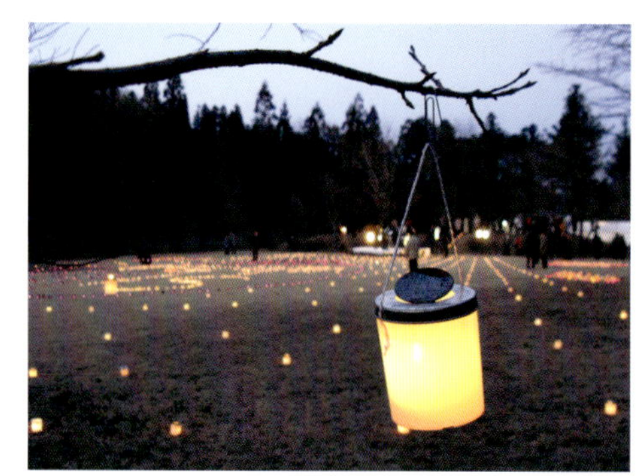
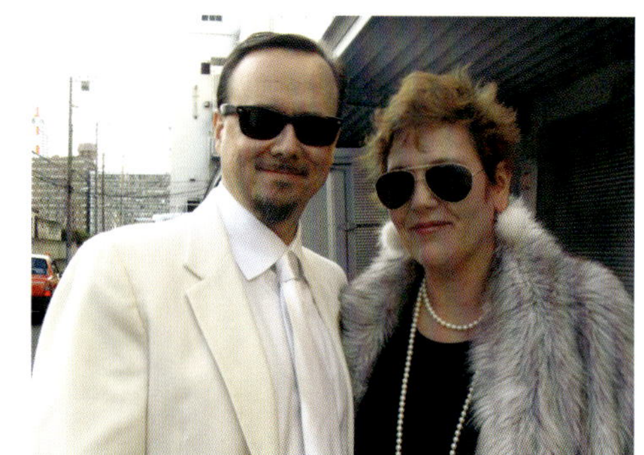
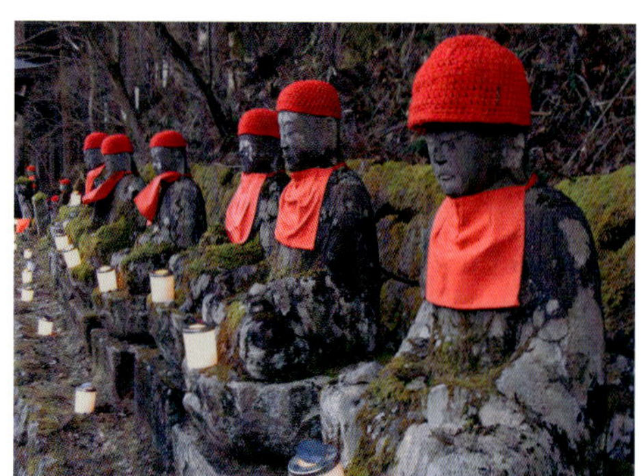
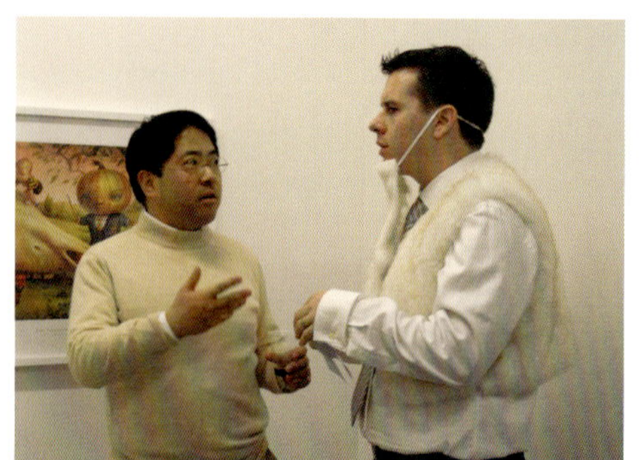
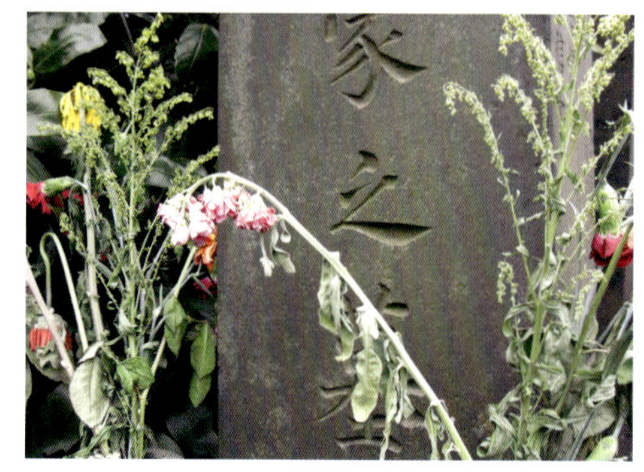
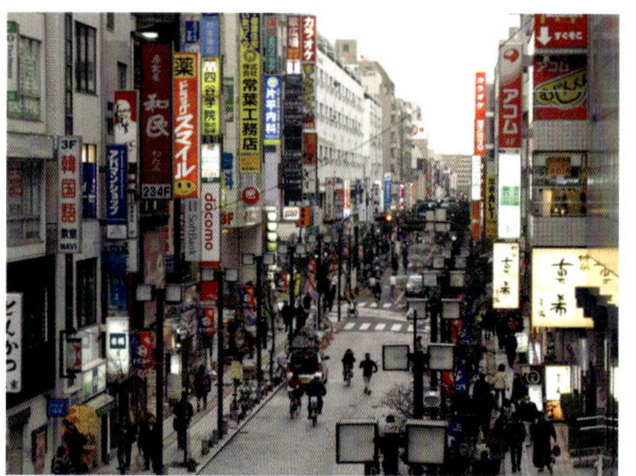
牛肉そば
¥1260（税込）
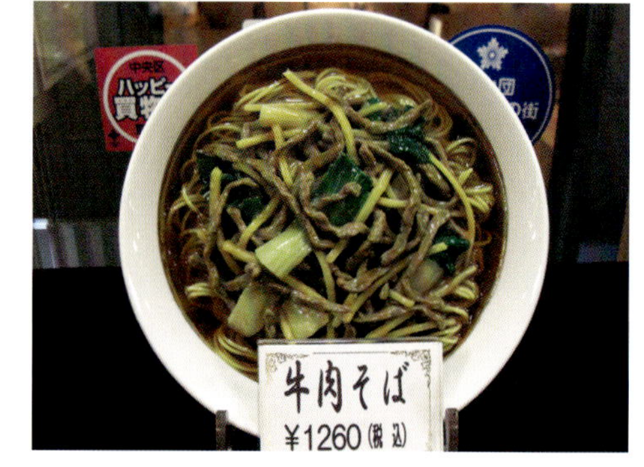
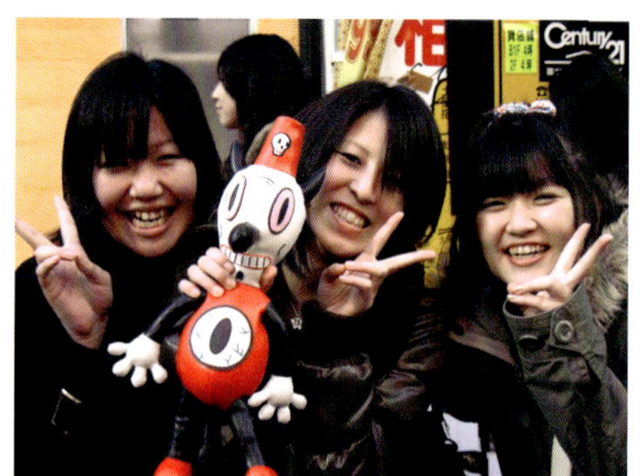
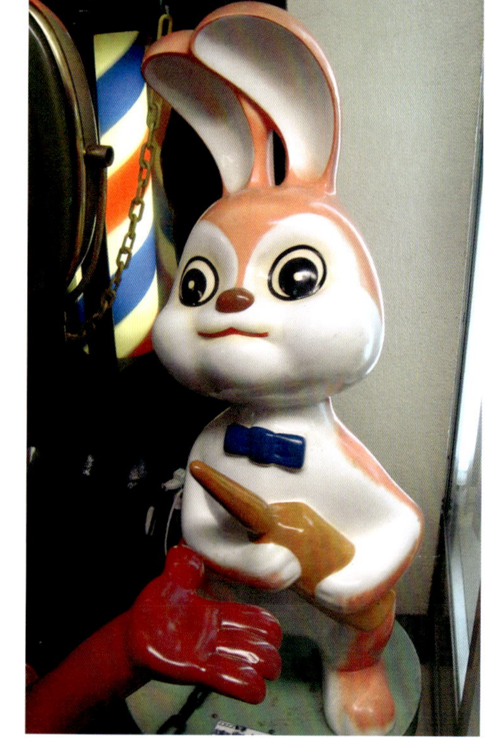
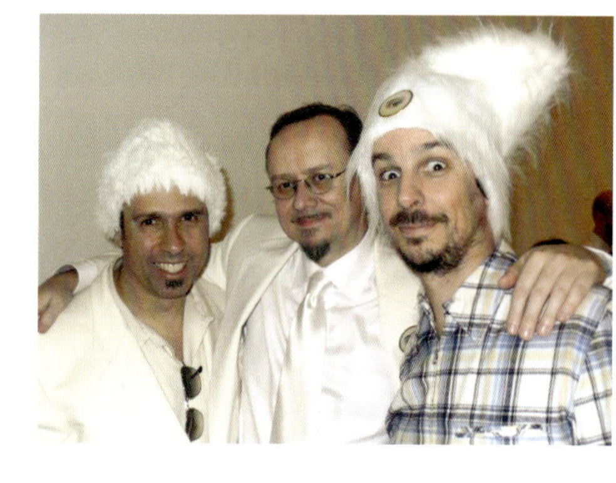
HOTEL P
ニューシャトー
全館 休憩 3,700 円均一
2人様
全館 宿泊 4,700 円均一
2人様
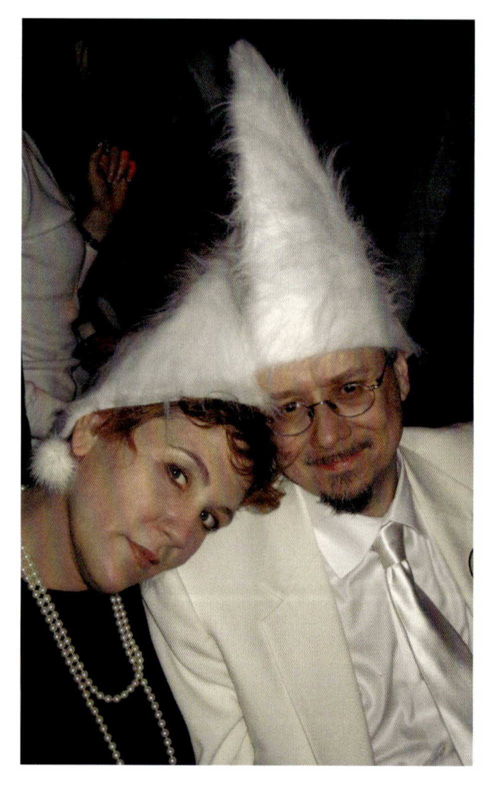
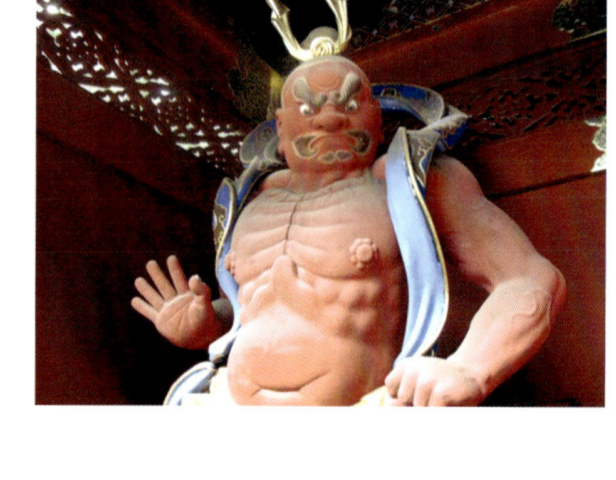
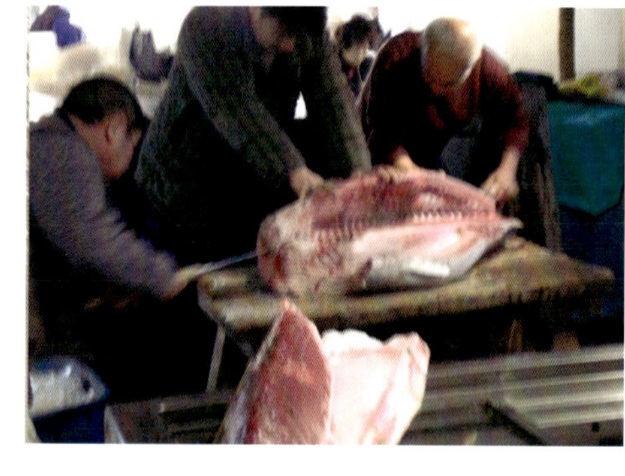
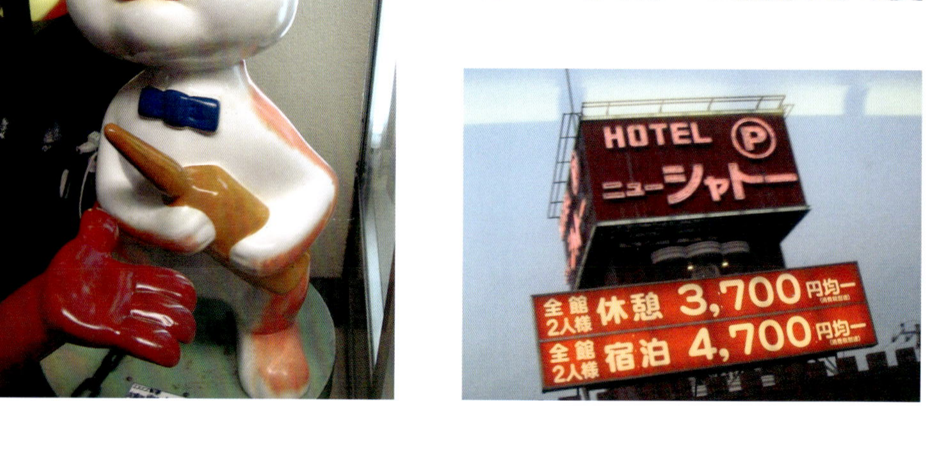
今日、モス気分。
MOS BURGER
宮崎名物
甘酢だれ仕立て
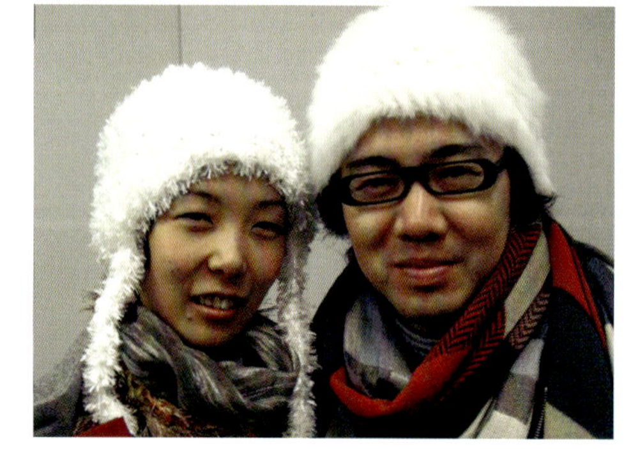
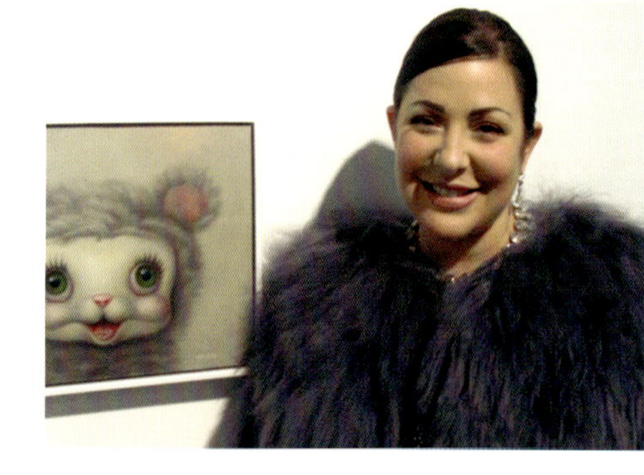
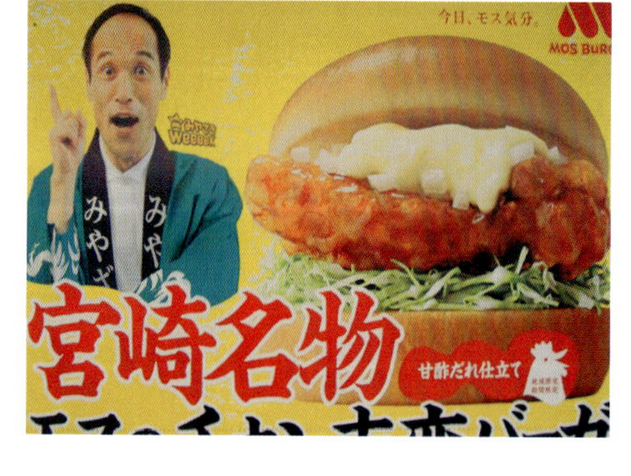
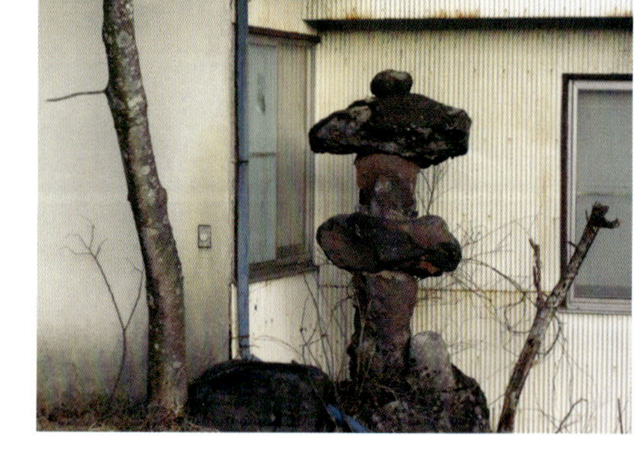
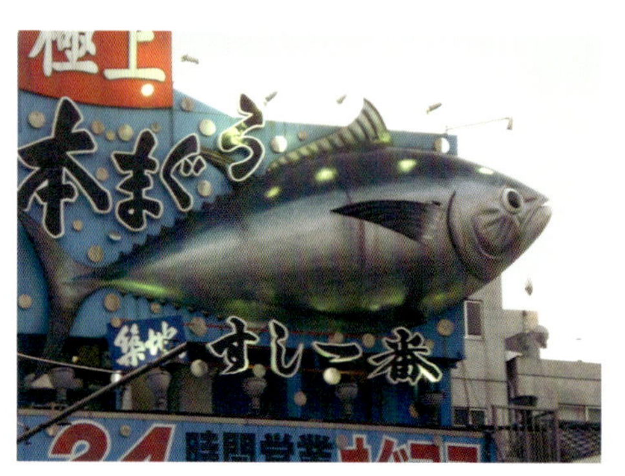
本まぐろ
すし一番
24 時間営業
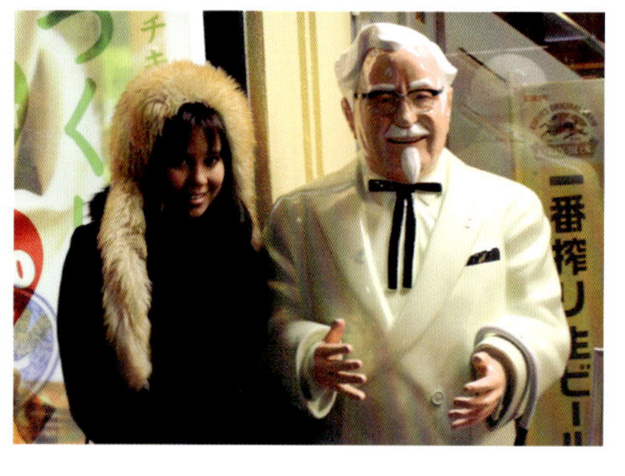
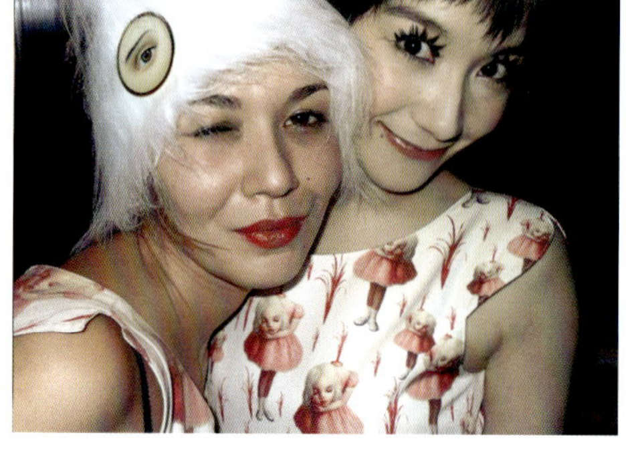
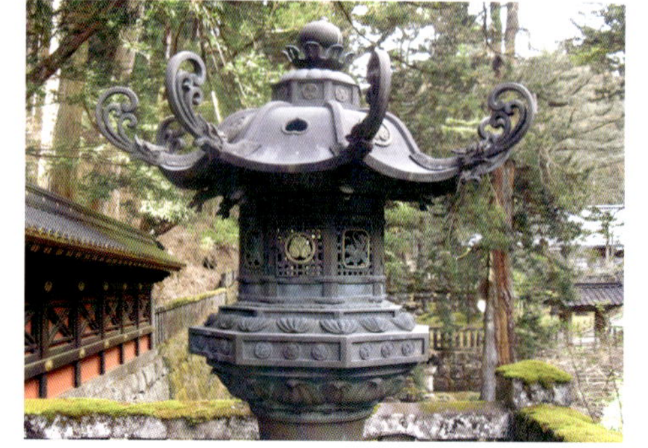
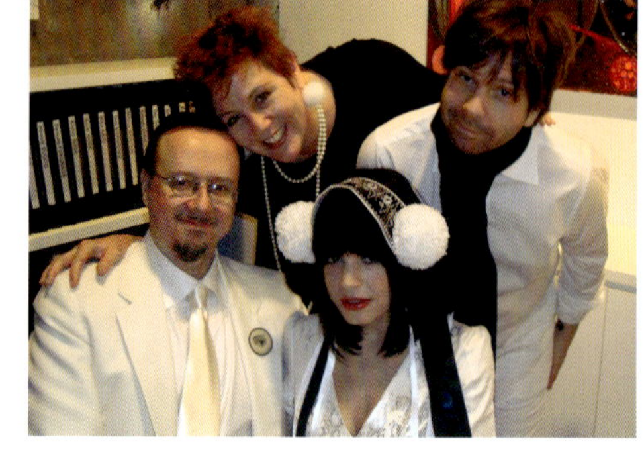

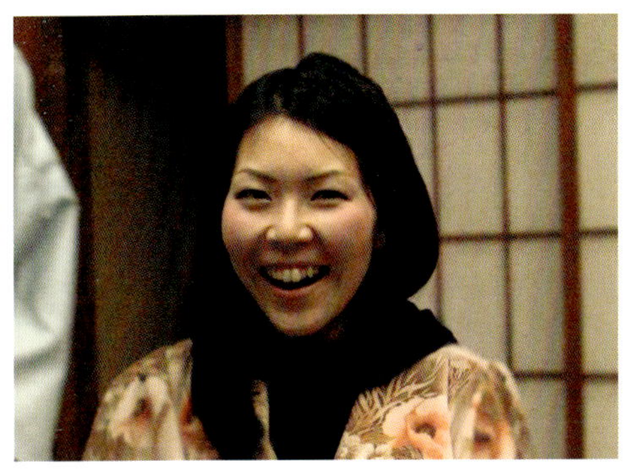
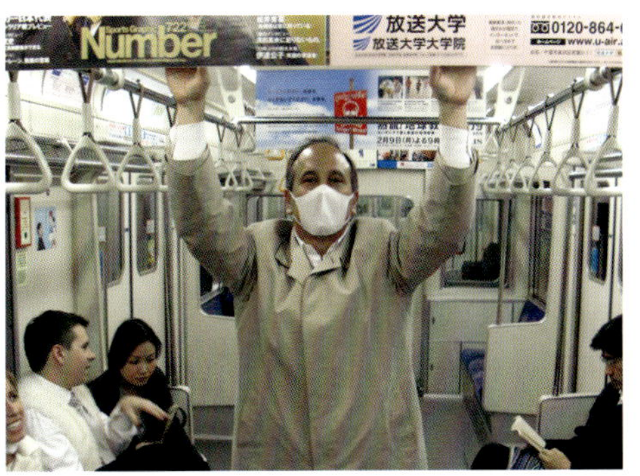
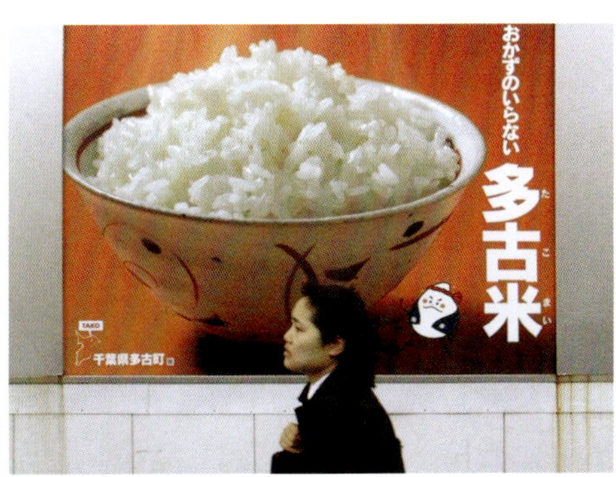
おかずのいらない
多古米
千葉県多古町
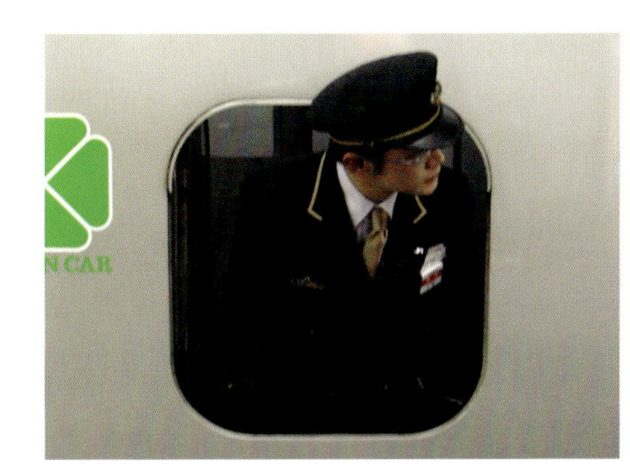
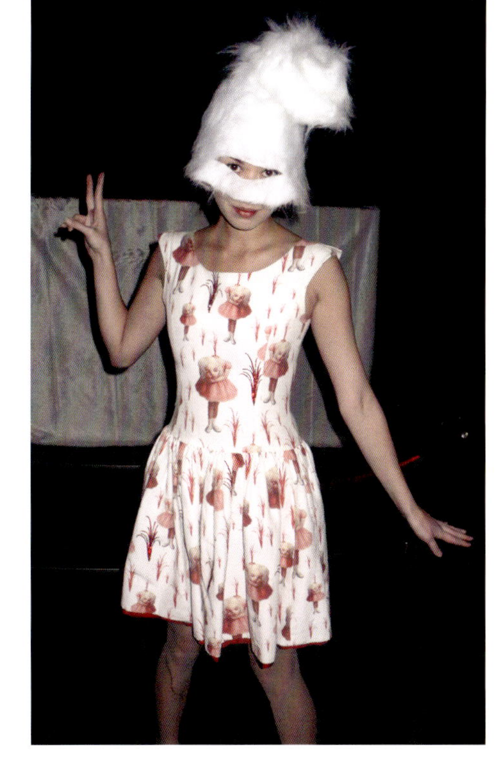
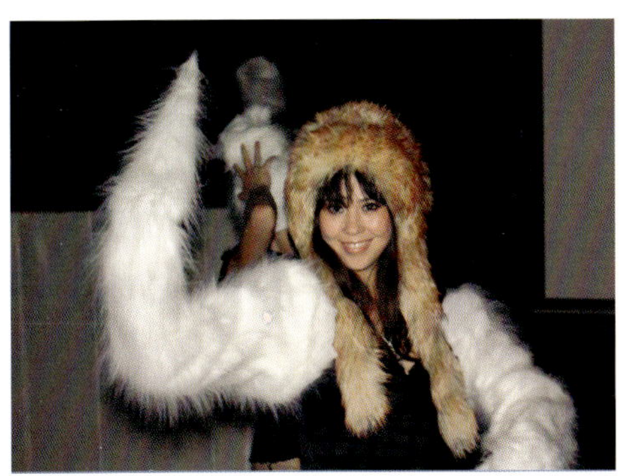
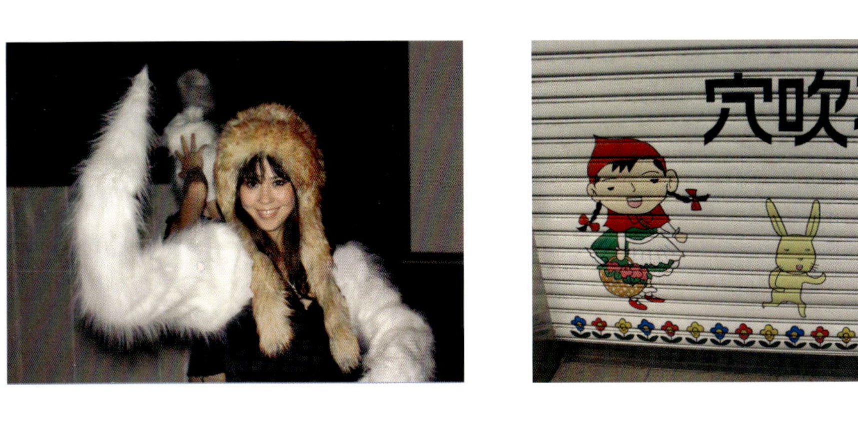
穴吹不動
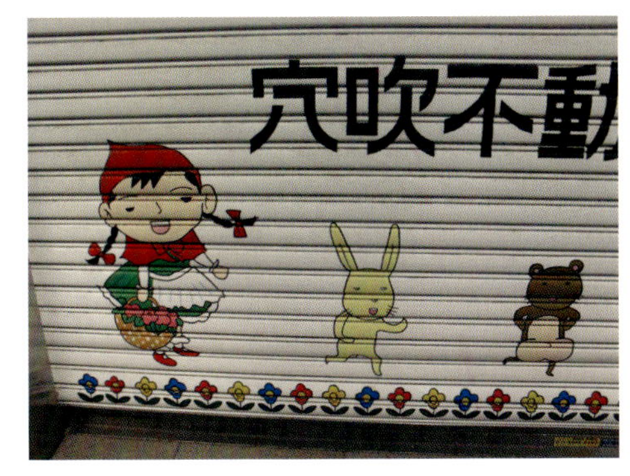
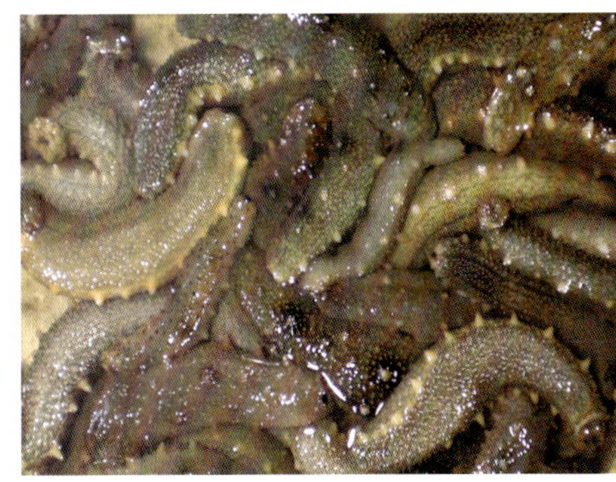
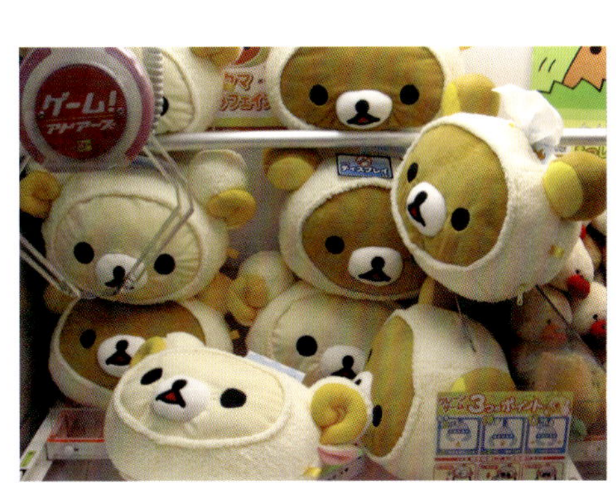
ゴールド
1200
さしみ
1,400
3枚下ろし
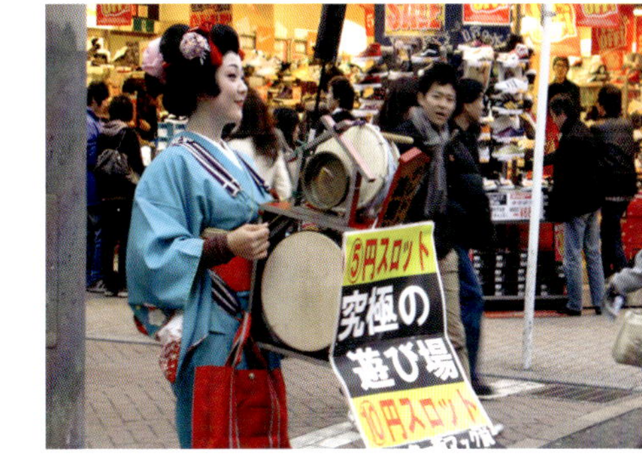
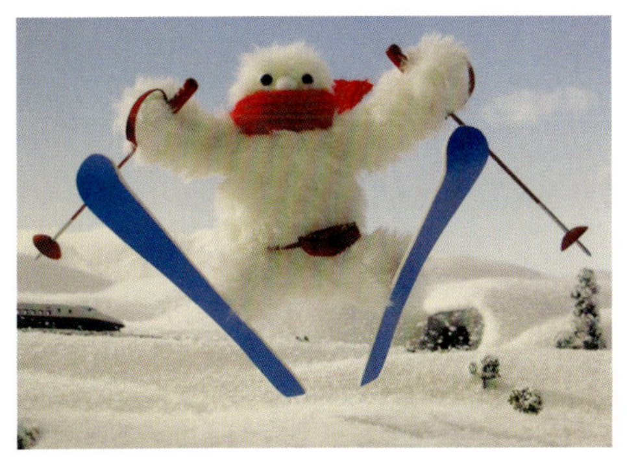
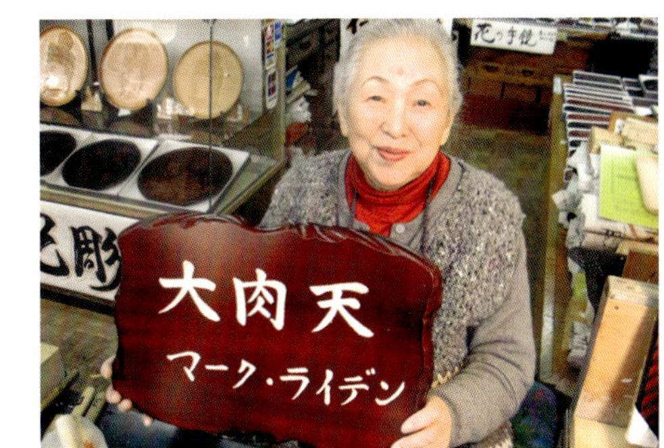
大肉天
マーク・ライデン
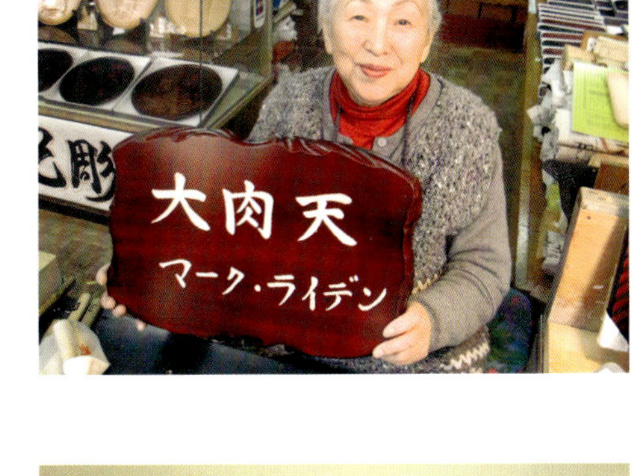
Suica
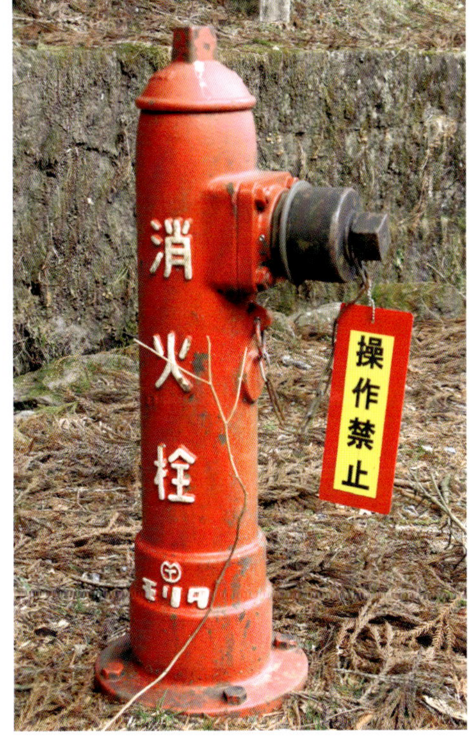
消火栓
操作禁止
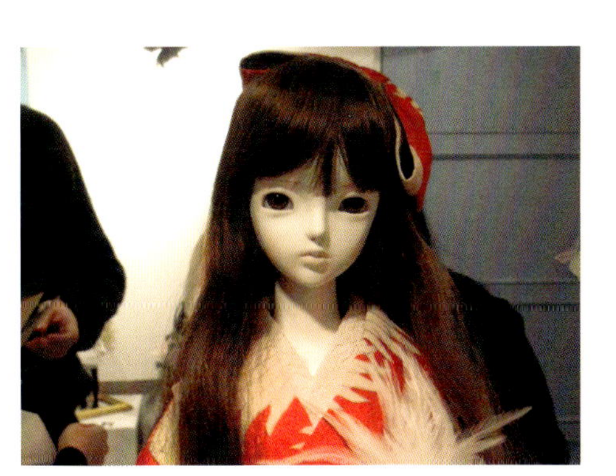
ゲーム!
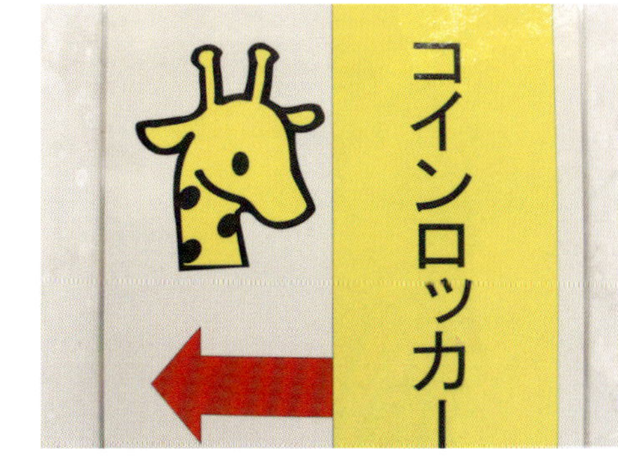
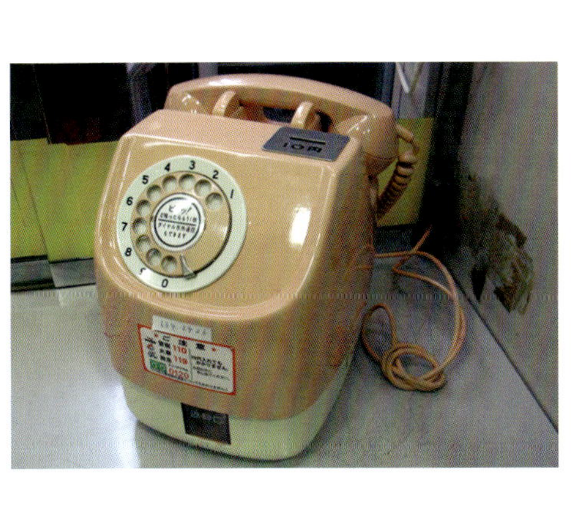
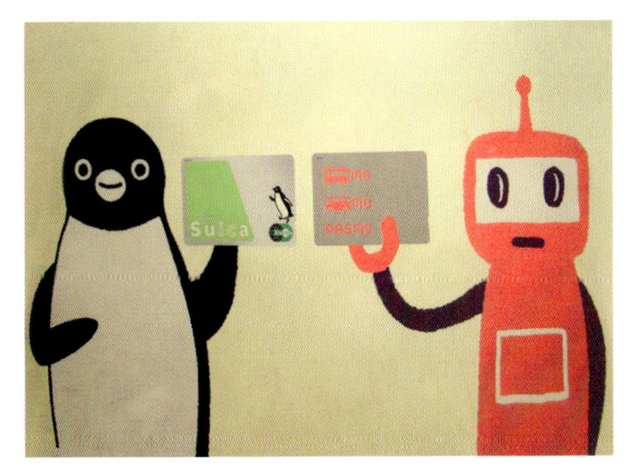
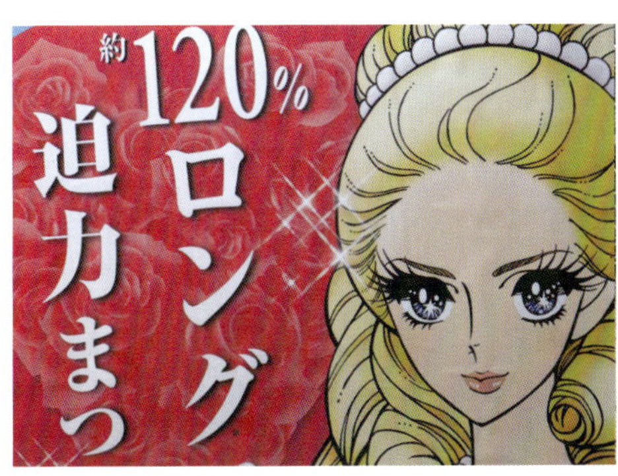
約120%
ロング
迫力
まつ
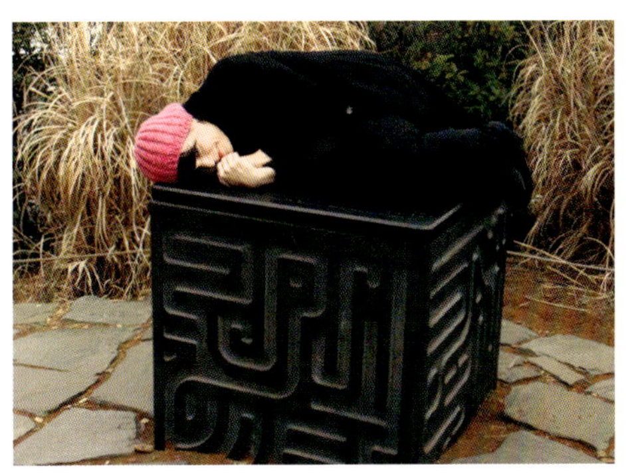
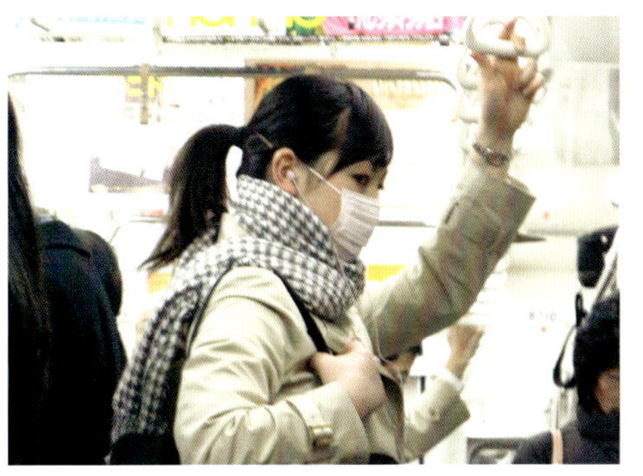
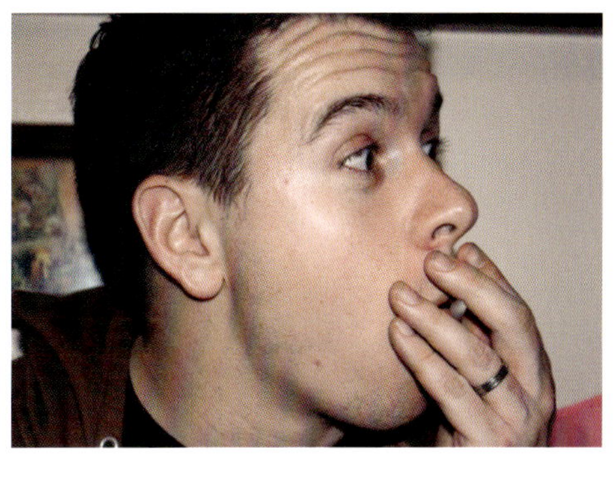
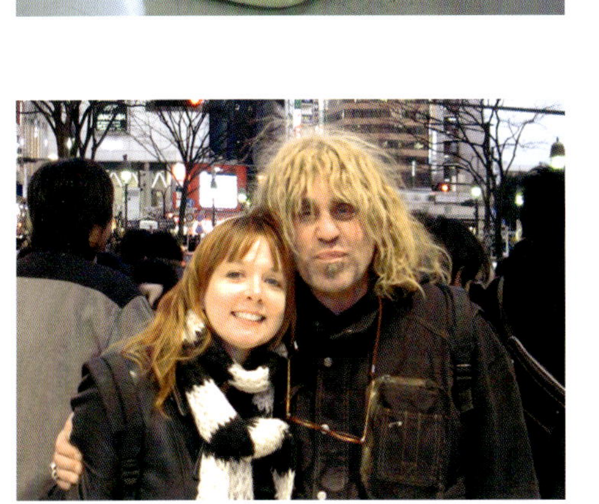

The Snow Yak Show
Mark Ryden

Tomio Koyama Gallery
February 7 – 28, 2009
Tokyo, Japan

Ronald E. Turner, Publisher
Colin S. Turner, Editor
Last Gasp of San Francisco
777 Florida Street
San Francisco, CA 94110 USA
Tel (415) 824-6636
www.lastgasp.com

Essay "Mark Ryden" by Yoshitomo Nara
Essay "Mark Ryden and the Snow Yak" by Kirsten Anderson

Designer: Makoto Yamamoto
Layout: Chris Long

The Japanese edition is published by PIE BOOKS, Tokyo.

First Edition

World English Edition   ISBN 978-0-86719-737-2

ザ スノーヤク ショー

2010年7月23日　初版第1刷発行

著者／ マーク ライデン

翻訳／ チャールズ ウォーゼン　清宮真理
アートディレクション／ 山本 誠
デザイン／ クリス ロング
日本語デザイン／ 柴 亜季子

協力／ 小山登美夫ギャラリー

発行人／ 三芳伸吾
発行元／ ピエ・ブックス
〒170-0005　東京都豊島区南大塚2-32-4
www.piebooks.com
営業　TEL 03-5395-4811　FAX 03-5395-4812　sales@piebooks.com
編集　TEL 03-5395-4820　FAX 03-5395-4821　editor@piebooks.com

ISBN 978-4-89444-861-2 C0071

本書は、2009年2月7日〜28日まで東京の小山登美夫ギャラリー www.tomiokoyamagallery.comで
開催されたマーク ライデン氏の個展「The Snow Yak Show」を契機に刊行されました。

© 2010 Mark Ryden
Printed in China

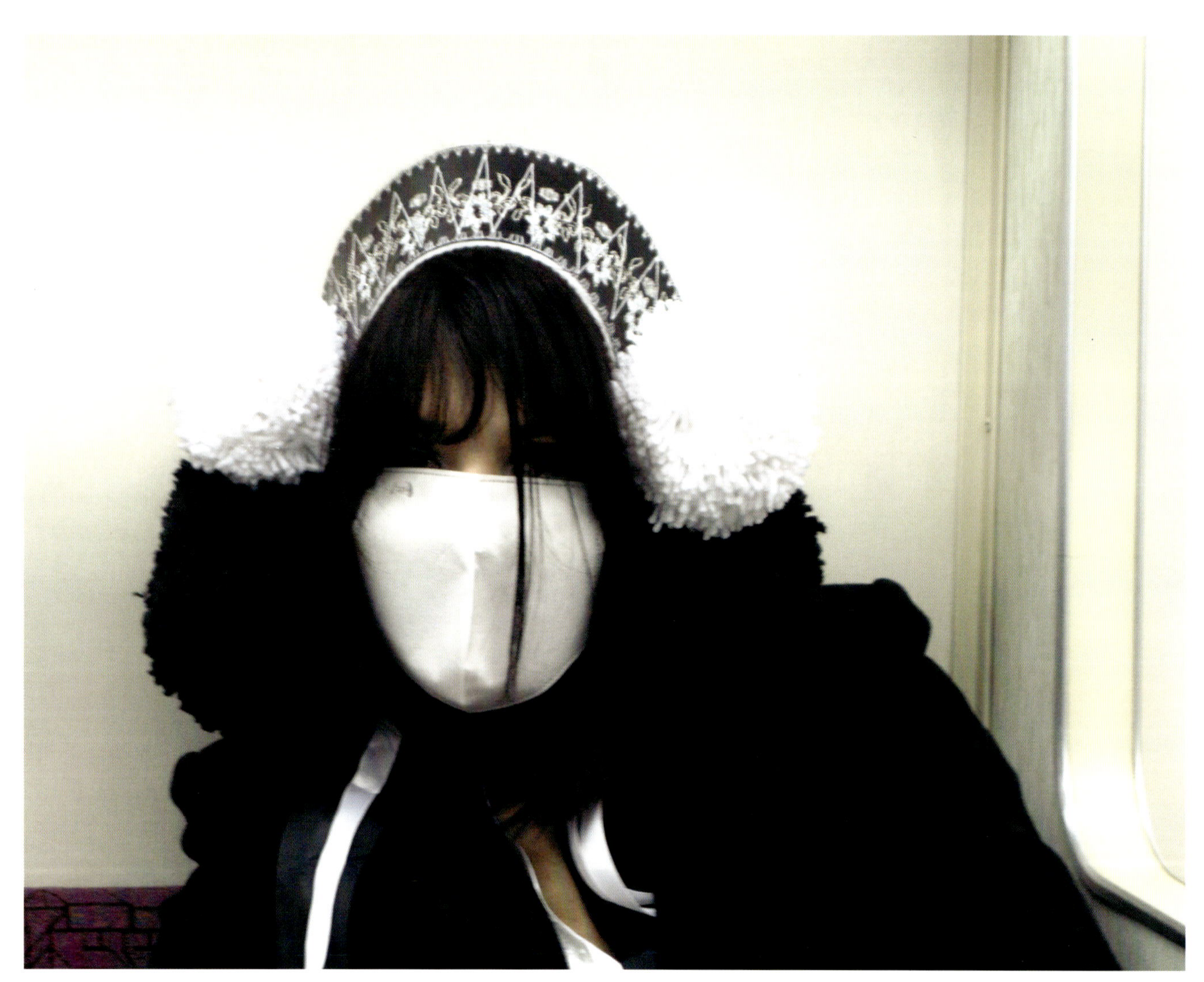